Proficiency Scales for the New Science Standards

A FRAMEWORK FOR SCIENCE
INSTRUCTION & ASSESSMENT

MARZANO
—Research—

Robert J. Marzano
David C. Yanoski
with **Diane E. Paynter**

555 North Morton Street
Bloomington, IN 47404
888.849.0851
FAX: 866.801.1447

email: info@marzanoresearch.com
marzanoresearch.com

Visit **marzanoresearch.com/reproducibles** to access materials related to this book.

Printed in the United States of America

Library of Congress Control Number: 2015908530

ISBN: 978-0-9903458-9-3 (paperback)

19 18   4 5

FSC
www.fsc.org
MIX
Paper from
responsible sources
FSC® C011935

Text and Cover Designer: Rachel Smith

Marzano Research
Development Team

Director of Publications

Julia A. Simms

Production Editor

Laurel Hecker

Editorial Assistants / Staff Writers

Ming Lee Newcomb

Elizabeth A. Bearden

Marzano Research Associates

Tina H. Boogren

Bev Clemens

Jane Doty Fischer

Jeff Flygare

Tammy Heflebower

Lynne Herr

Mitzi Hoback

Jan K. Hoegh

Jeanie Iberlin

Russell Jenson

Jessica Kanold-McIntyre

Bettina Kates

Sonny Magaña

Margaret McInteer

Diane E. Paynter

Kristin Poage

Salle Quackenboss

Cameron Rains

Tom Roy

Mike Ruyle

Gerry Varty

Phil Warrick

Kenneth C. Williams

Visit **marzanoresearch.com/reproducibles** to access materials related to this book.

Table of Contents

Part I: Applying the New Science Standards

Part II: Scoring the New Science Standards

About the Authors

Robert J. Marzano, PhD, is the cofounder and CEO of Marzano Research in Denver, Colorado. During his forty-seven years in the field of education, he has worked with educators as a speaker and trainer and has authored more than forty books and 250 articles on topics such as instruction, assessment, writing and implementing standards, cognition, effective leadership, and school intervention. His books include *The Art and Science of Teaching*, *Leaders of Learning*, *On Excellence in Teaching*, *Effective Supervision*, *The Classroom Strategies Series*, *Using Common Core Standards to Enhance Classroom Instruction and Assessment*, *Vocabulary for the Common Core*, *Vocabulary for the New Science Standards*, *Teacher Evaluation That Makes a Difference*, *A Handbook for High Reliability Schools*, *Awaken the Learner*, and *Managing the Inner World of Teaching*. His practical translations of the most current research and theory into classroom strategies are known internationally and are widely practiced by both teachers and administrators. He received a bachelor's degree from Iona College in New York, a master's degree from Seattle University, and a doctorate from the University of Washington.

David C. Yanoski, MA, is associate director of research and development for Marzano Research in Denver, Colorado. He has worked in K–12 education as a classroom teacher, mentor coach, and teacher leader and has served on curriculum and assessment development teams. He has facilitated the development of proficiency scales with state departments of education, schools, and districts across the United States. He received his bachelor's degree from Midland University in Fremont, Nebraska, and a master's degree in education from the University of Phoenix.

Diane E. Paynter, MA, is the director of curriculum development for Marzano Research in Denver, Colorado. She has worked extensively in the areas of standards, curriculum and instruction, assessment, grading, record keeping, literacy development, and leadership. She is the author and coauthor of many works including *For the Love of Words*, *A Handbook for Classroom Instruction That Works*, and *The Pathfinder Project*. She is also a member of the ASCD national cadre focusing on the implementation of research from Dr. Robert J. Marzano's book *The Art and Science of Teaching*. She received her bachelor's degree from Brigham Young University and a master's degree from Oakland City University.

About Marzano Research

Marzano Research is a joint venture between Solution Tree and Dr. Robert J. Marzano. Marzano Research combines Dr. Marzano's forty years of educational research with continuous action research in all major areas of schooling in order to provide effective and accessible instructional strategies, leadership strategies, and classroom assessment strategies that are always at the forefront of best practice. By providing such an all-inclusive research-into-practice resource center, Marzano Research provides teachers and principals with the tools they need to effect profound and immediate improvement in student achievement.

Part I

Applying the New Science Standards

1

The Evolution of Standards-Based Education in Science

In previous decades, educators in the United States called for K–12 science standards that schools could broadly implement across the country. These requests ultimately prompted the development of comprehensive science standards such as the National Research Council's (NRC; 1996) *National Science Education Standards* (NSES) and the American Association for the Advancement of Science's (AAAS) *Benchmarks for Science Literacy* (1993, 2009). These documents enjoyed extensive use and adaptation throughout the U.S. and often guided the development of individual state science standards (Colorado Department of Education, 2009; Massachusetts Department of Education, 2006; Minnesota Department of Education, 2009; Wyoming State Board of Education, 2008).

However, the NSES and the AAAS *Benchmarks* were originally published in 1996 and 1993 respectively. In 2010, the release of the widely adopted Common Core State Standards (CCSS) in English language arts (ELA; National Governors Association Center for Best Practices & Council of Chief State School Officers [NGA & CCSSO], 2010a) and mathematics (NGA & CCSSO, 2010b) confirmed that these previous science standards documents needed to be updated. As Achieve (n.d.a) noted, during the fifteen-year period between the publication of both science standards documents and the CCSS, "major advances in science" warranted adjustments to K–12 science instruction. Aside from the demand for an up-to-date curriculum, new science standards were needed for at least four additional reasons.

1. Reduced economic competitiveness of the U.S., including decreases in U.S. patent applications and technology exports (National Science Board, 2012)

2. Comparatively low or average performance of U.S. students on international reading, science, and mathematics assessments (Fleischman, Hopstock, Pelczar, & Shelley, 2010) and in terms of high school graduation rates (Organisation for Economic Co-operation and Development, 2012)

3. Low academic achievement of U.S. students in science (National Center for Education Statistics, 2012)

4. Low rates of scientific and technological literacy among U.S. adults (Miller, 2010)

The NRC (2012) added to the call for updated science standards, noting that "understanding science and engineering, now more than ever, is essential for every American citizen" (p. 7). As evidence, the organization pointed to "everyday decisions" (2012, p. 7) such as interpreting water policy or choosing between medical treatments—relatively common decisions for many Americans. According to the NRC, K–12 science education in the U.S. had failed to prepare Americans for these situations.

These concerns, among others, incited widespread re-evaluation of the way the U.S. approaches science education. Ultimately, these doubts spurred an effort to develop a new, common set of science standards—"the first broad national recommendations for science instruction since 1996" (Gillis, 2013). This broad initiative was named the Next Generation Science Standards* (NGSS Lead States, 2013).

The Next Generation Science Standards Initiative

The three-year process of forging the Next Generation Science Standards (NGSS) began with the partnership of four prominent organizations in the fields of education and science.

1. The National Research Council (NRC), a nonprofit organization that produced the *National Science Education Standards* (NSES) in 1996

2. The American Association for the Advancement of Science (AAAS), a nonprofit organization that produced the *Benchmarks for Science Literacy* in 1993

3. Achieve, a nonprofit education reform organization that partnered with the National Governors Association and Council of Chief State School Officers (NGA & CCSSO; 2010a, 2010b) to produce the Common Core State Standards (CCSS) in 2010

4. The National Science Teachers Association (NSTA), an organization of science teachers, science supervisors, administrators, scientists, and business and industry representatives dedicated to improving science education in the U.S.

These four partner organizations collaborated at various stages of the development process to create the NGSS. Table 1.1 depicts an overview of this process.

Table 1.1: Development Process of the Next Generation Science Standards

Development Stage	Time Period	Development Steps
Conceptualization	2009–2012	• The NRC, AAAS, Achieve, and NSTA teamed up to develop the NGSS. • Achieve (2010) published its *International Science Benchmarking Report*. • The NRC (2012) published *A Framework for K–12 Science Education* after multiple rounds of revision.
Writing	2012–2013	• Using the NRC (2012) framework as a guide, Achieve managed twenty-six lead states and forty-one writers and reviewers as they drafted the NGSS. • Achieve released two public drafts of the NGSS (one in May 2012 and one in January 2013) for web-based review and feedback. • The AAAS, the NSTA, state leaders, K–12 teachers, professors, and scientists reviewed the NGSS draft and offered feedback. • The NRC conducted an independent review of the NGSS to ensure alignment to its framework. • Achieve published the final version of the NGSS in April 2013.

Source: Adapted from Henderson, 2013.

As shown in table 1.1, the formation of the NGSS proceeded in two main phases: (1) conceptualization and (2) writing. Here, we briefly describe each phase.

Conceptualization of the NGSS

Unlike the CCSS, which were conceived, drafted, and published in a period of about one year, initial writing of the NGSS did not begin until 2011, two years after the project's inception. Instead, the process of creating the NGSS began with an extensive foundational period of research and theorizing that occurred in two stages: (1) international benchmarking and (2) creation of the NRC framework.

International Benchmarking

Achieve (2010) took the first step in developing the NGSS by using an analytical method called *benchmarking*. In business, benchmarking is the practice of comparing a company's procedures and expectations to those of highly successful companies or to a set of industrywide best practices. This allows a business to identify which areas need attention in order to improve overall performance. Educational benchmarking applies this same principle to a classroom, school, or district. For example, throughout a school year, a district might conduct benchmark assessments to help teachers monitor student progress or modify their instruction. A district or an individual school could also perform benchmark analyses of high-performing schools to identify areas it can improve within its own system.

Achieve's (2010) process of international benchmarking involved reviewing and evaluating science standards from other countries around the world. The overall goal of the international benchmarking study, according to Achieve (2010), was to "inform the development" (p. 3) of the NGSS. Achieve (n.d.e) summarized the benefits of international benchmarking:

> International benchmarking is important from a national perspective to ensure our long-term economic competitiveness. Many feel it is necessary for American students to be held to the same academic expectations as students in other countries. The successes of other nations can provide potential guidance for decision-making in the United States.

However, international benchmarking does not simply involve copying the standards of high-performing nations. Instead, Achieve (2010) recommended that results of its study be used as guidelines during the process of standards development, rather than strict rules that must be followed or replicated:

> International benchmarking does not mean that the United States should simply emulate other countries' standards. In recent years, the United States has made significant strides in advancing the research base that underpins science education and also has its own exemplars. It is also the case that there are shortcomings in all of the standards Achieve examined that are equally instructive for improving standards. (p. 9)

Achieve's (2010) international benchmarking study involved a quantitative and qualitative review of the science standards from specific countries with particularly strong performance on international assessments or of special interest to the United States (Achieve, n.d.e). The quantitative component included an analysis of the science content and skills in each nation's standards, which yielded the four key findings shown in table 1.2 (page 6).

Table 1.2: Four Key Findings of Achieve's Quantitative International Benchmarking Analysis

Finding #1	All countries required participation in integrated science instruction through the lower secondary level. Seven of ten countries continued that instruction through grade 10, providing a strong foundation in scientific literacy.
Finding #2	Content standards in other countries focused most heavily on biology and physical sciences (physics and chemistry content taken together) and least heavily on Earth and space sciences.
Finding #3	Other countries' standards focused life science instruction strongly on human biology and relationships among living things in a way that highlighted the personal and social significance of life science for students.
Finding #4	Crosscutting content common to all of the sciences (such as the nature of science, the nature of technology, and engineering) received considerable attention, as did the development of inquiry skills at the primary level and advanced inquiry skills at the lower secondary level.

Source: Adapted from Achieve, 2010, pp. 2–3.

In the qualitative component of the study, Achieve (n.d.d) identified the following features of effective science standards:

- The use of an overarching conceptual framework
- Clarification statements to provide examples that clarify the level of rigor expected and connect concepts with applications
- Concrete links between standards and assessments
- Development of inquiry and design processes in parallel to facilitate students engaging in both science and engineering practices

Traces of all four of these features were observable in the final version of the NGSS. Nonetheless, the first element—use of an overarching conceptual framework—had perhaps the most direct influence on the development of the standards. It manifested as *A Framework for K–12 Science Education: Practices, Crosscutting Concepts, and Core Ideas* (NRC, 2012).

Creation of the NRC Framework

In January of 2010, the NRC convened a group of eighteen experts in science, engineering, cognitive science, teaching and learning, curriculum, assessment, and education policy. Together, the NRC committee set out to create a conceptual framework for science education, which the committee described as

> a broad description of the content and sequence of learning expected of all students by the completion of high school—but not at the level of detail of grade-by-grade standards or, at the high school level, course descriptions and standards. (NRC, 2012, p. 8)

In other words, the committee did not draft actual standards. Rather, the NRC identified the most important aspects of a competitive science curriculum and articulated these elements across grades K–12 with the intention that the framework would guide the drafting of new science standards.

To begin the process of creating its framework, the NRC committee contracted four design teams—comprised primarily of professors and university faculty—to focus on four scientific disciplines: (1) physical sciences, (2) life sciences, (3) Earth and space sciences, and (4) engineering, technology, and the applications of science. Each design team reviewed the "relevant research on learning and teaching" (NRC, 2012, p. 17) in its respective scientific discipline. The design teams also considered content and skills articulated in previous science standards documents, such as the NRC's (1996) NSES, the AAAS's (1993, 2009) *Benchmarks*, the National Assessment Governing Board's (2008) *Science Framework for the 2009 National Assessment of Educational Progress*, and the College Board's (2009) *Standards for*

College Success in science. Using this research to inform their work, the design teams drafted sections of the framework, presented them to the NRC committee, and revised the drafts according to committee feedback.

This process continued until the summer of 2010, when the NRC posted the first draft of its framework online and invited the public to ask questions and offer comments. In addition to collecting online feedback from over two thousand people, the NSTA and the AAAS coordinated focus-group response sessions and solicited reactions from science and engineering organizations and experts across the country (NRC, 2012). Over the next several months, the NRC committee used this feedback to make "substantial revisions" (NRC, 2012, p. 18) to the document draft. One year later, in July of 2012, the NRC published the final version of *A Framework for K–12 Science Education: Practices, Crosscutting Concepts, and Core Ideas.*

Writing the NGSS

To begin the writing process, Achieve invited all fifty states to apply to become one of the NGSS lead states. In the end, the following twenty-six states joined together to draft the new science standards (Achieve, n.d.f).

1. Arizona	10. Maine	19. Ohio
2. Arkansas	11. Maryland	20. Oregon
3. California	12. Massachusetts	21. Rhode Island
4. Delaware	13. Michigan	22. South Dakota
5. Georgia	14. Minnesota	23. Tennessee
6. Illinois	15. Montana	24. Vermont
7. Iowa	16. New Jersey	25. Washington
8. Kansas	17. New York	26. West Virginia
9. Kentucky	18. North Carolina	

Each state assembled a group of writers and reviewers from a variety of scientific, educational, and business communities to help draft the standards. The forty-one-member writing team included K–12 science teachers, experts in special education and English language acquisition, state standards and assessment developers, business and industry professionals, and workforce development specialists (Achieve, n.d.i). Though Achieve facilitated these individuals and the twenty-six lead states' work, the organization did not draft the standards themselves. Instead, Achieve "played a similar role" (Robelen, 2012) to its part in coordinating the development of the CCSS. Also note that the federal government did not fund the development of the NGSS (Achieve, n.d.d). Instead, private foundations such as the Carnegie Corporation of New York, the Noyce Foundation, the Cisco Foundation, and DuPont provided funding (Gillis, 2013).

While composing the standards, the writing team conducted several rounds of review, feedback, and revision. Figure 1.1 depicts the general process and timeline for writing the NGSS.

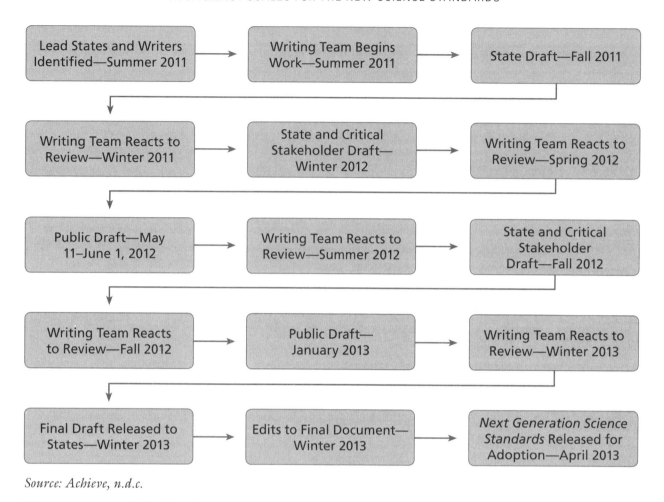

Source: Achieve, n.d.c.

Figure 1.1: General timeline for the creation of the Next Generation Science Standards.

Emulating the actions of the NRC in the construction of its framework and the NGA and CCSSO in the construction of the CCSS, Achieve and the NGSS lead states welcomed feedback from various parties. As indicated in figure 1.1, the NGSS went through two rounds of public feedback: one in May 2012 and one in January 2013. The writing team also received feedback from specific individuals and organizations—which Achieve (n.d.b) called "critical stakeholders"—that they believed had a special interest in the NGSS. These individuals included representatives from the AAAS and the NSTA, state leaders, K–12 teachers, professors, and scientists, as well as experts in postsecondary education, state standards and assessments, mathematics and literacy, business and industry, workforce development, education policy, special education, and English language acquisition (Achieve, n.d.b). Finally, all fifty states had the chance to read and offer feedback on preliminary drafts of the standards (Achieve, n.d.g).

In April 2013, the final version of the NGSS was published. Several features set the NGSS apart from previous standards documents for science education, prompting writing team member Joseph S. Krajcik to proclaim, "You can travel worldwide and you're not going to find standards like them" (quoted in Robelen, 2013). These unique characteristics as well as an overview of the initial reception of the NGSS are described online at **marzanoresearch.com/reproducibles**.

The Influence of the NRC Framework

It is important to keep in mind that *A Framework for K–12 Science Education: Practices, Crosscutting Concepts, and Core Ideas* (NRC, 2012) heavily informed the creation of the NGSS. As stated previously, the NRC framework was written before the NGSS with the intention of determining the critical content the standards themselves should contain. The framework divided this content into three dimensions: (1) scientific and engineering practices, (2) crosscutting concepts, and (3) disciplinary core ideas. Table 1.3 lists the three dimensions and their component parts.

Table 1.3: The Three Dimensions of the NRC Framework

Scientific and Engineering Practices	1. Asking questions (for science) and defining problems (for engineering) 2. Developing and using models 3. Planning and carrying out investigations 4. Analyzing and interpreting data 5. Using mathematics and computational thinking 6. Constructing explanations (for science) and designing solutions (for engineering) 7. Engaging in argument from evidence 8. Obtaining, evaluating, and communicating information
Crosscutting Concepts	1. Patterns 2. Cause and effect: Mechanism and explanation 3. Scale, proportion, and quantity 4. Systems and system models 5. Energy and matter: Flows, cycles, and conservation 6. Structure and function 7. Stability and change
Disciplinary Core Ideas	*Physical Sciences* PS1: Matter and its interactions PS2: Motion and stability: Forces and interactions PS3: Energy PS4: Waves and their applications in technologies for information transfer *Life Sciences* LS1: From molecules to organisms: Structures and processes LS2: Ecosystems: Interactions, energy, and dynamics LS3: Heredity: Inheritance and variation of traits LS4: Biological evolution: Unity and diversity *Earth and Space Sciences* ESS1: Earth's place in the universe ESS2: Earth's systems ESS3: Earth and human activity *Engineering, Technology, and Applications of Science* ETS1: Engineering design ETS2: Links among engineering, technology, science, and society

Source: NRC, 2012, p. 3.

The first dimension included scientific and engineering practices, which were defined as "behaviors that scientists engage in as they investigate and build models and theories about the natural world" (Achieve, n.d.h). The second dimension contained crosscutting concepts, which were defined as concepts that "bridge disciplinary boundaries [and have] explanatory value throughout much of science and engineering" (NRC, 2012, p. 83). (We recommend addressing the crosscutting concepts through vocabulary instruction, as detailed in the book *Vocabulary for the New Science Standards* [Marzano, Rogers, & Simms, 2015].) The third dimension was composed of disciplinary core ideas (DCIs), which were defined as ideas that "focus K–12 science curriculum, instruction and assessments on the most important aspects of science" (Achieve, n.d.h). Within the third dimension, the NRC identified four scientific disciplines: (1) physical sciences, (2) life sciences, (3) Earth and space sciences, and (4) engineering, technology, and applications of science. Each discipline contained core ideas, which specified areas of knowledge within the discipline with which students should become familiar. Table 1.4 shows how sub-ideas further divide each core idea.

Table 1.4: Core and Sub-Ideas Within the Four Scientific Disciplines

Physical Sciences	Life Sciences	Earth and Space Sciences	Engineering, Technology, and Applications of Science
Core Idea PS1: Matter and Its Interactions PS1.A: Structure and Properties of Matter PS1.B: Chemical Reactions PS1.C: Nuclear Processes **Core Idea PS2: Motion and Stability: Forces and Interactions** PS2.A: Forces and Motion PS2.B: Types of Interactions PS2.C: Stability and Instability in Physical Systems **Core Idea PS3: Energy** PS3.A: Definitions of Energy PS3.B: Conservation of Energy and Energy Transfer PS3.C: Relationship Between Energy and Forces PS3.D: Energy in Chemical Processes and Everyday Life **Core Idea PS4: Waves and Their Applications in Technologies for Information Transfer** PS4.A: Wave Properties PS4.B: Electromagnetic Radiation PS4.C: Information Technologies and Instrumentation	**Core Idea LS1: From Molecules to Organisms: Structures and Processes** LS1.A: Structure and Function LS1.B: Growth and Development of Organisms LS1.C: Organization for Matter and Energy Flow in Organisms LS1.D: Information Processing **Core Idea LS2: Ecosystems: Interactions, Energy, and Dynamics** LS2.A: Interdependent Relationships in Ecosystems LS2.B: Cycles of Matter and Energy Transfer in Ecosystems LS2.C: Ecosystem Dynamics, Functioning, and Resilience LS2.D: Social Interactions and Group Behavior **Core Idea LS3: Heredity: Inheritance and Variation of Traits** LS3.A: Inheritance of Traits LS3.B: Variation of Traits **Core Idea LS4: Biological Evolution: Unity and Diversity** LS4.A: Evidence of Common Ancestry and Diversity LS4.B: Natural Selection LS4.C: Adaptation LS4.D: Biodiversity and Humans	**Core Idea ESS1: Earth's Place in the Universe** ESS1.A: The Universe and Its Stars ESS1.B: Earth and the Solar System ESS1.C: The History of Planet Earth **Core Idea ESS2: Earth's Systems** ESS2.A: Earth Materials and Systems ESS2.B: Plate Tectonics and Large-Scale System Interactions ESS2.C: The Roles of Water in Earth's Surface Processes ESS2.D: Weather and Climate ESS2.E: Biogeology **Core Idea ESS3: Earth and Human Activity** ESS3.A: Natural Resources ESS3.B: Natural Hazards ESS3.C: Human Impacts on Earth Systems ESS3.D: Global Climate Change	**Core Idea ETS1: Engineering Design** ETS1.A: Defining and Delimiting an Engineering Problem ETS1.B: Developing Possible Solutions ETS1.C: Optimizing the Design Solution **Core Idea ETS2: Links Among Engineering, Technology, Science, and Society** ETS2.A: Interdependence of Science, Engineering, and Technology ETS2.B: Influence of Engineering, Technology, and Science on Society and the Natural World

Source: NRC, 2012, pp. 105, 142, 171, 203.

It is important to note that the organizational structure of the NGSS mirrored the order of the core ideas from the framework listed in table 1.4, as content knowledge—disciplinary core ideas—organized the standards rather than either of the other two dimensions (scientific and engineering practices or crosscutting concepts).

Though the NRC (2012) defined the three dimensions separately, it recommended that "in order to facilitate students' learning, the dimensions . . . be woven together in standards, curricula, instruction, and assessments" (pp. 29–30). To accomplish such an amalgamation, the NGSS used *performance expectations*. Each performance expectation in the NGSS was a synthesis of related elements from the three dimensions. As depicted in figure 1.2, each NGSS standard has three sections: (1) a performance expectations section, (2) foundation boxes, and (3) a connections section.

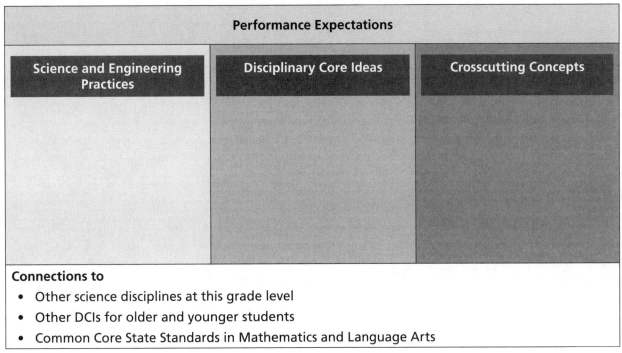

Source: Achieve, 2013b, p. 1.

Figure 1.2: Generic format of an NGSS standard.

The first section contains *performance expectations*, grade-specific statements that serve as an indication of a student's proficiency with related knowledge and skills. These statements were considered the leading edge of the NGSS. Some performance expectations have clarification statements, which are specific examples of how the performance expectation manifests in the classroom, or assessment boundaries, which limit the scope of a performance expectation. The three foundation boxes below the performance expectation section represent each of the three dimensions of the framework, with science and engineering practices in the box on the left, disciplinary core ideas in the center box, and crosscutting concepts in the box on the right. The elements within the foundation boxes were eventually "combined to produce the performance expectations (PEs)" found in each standard (Achieve, 2013b, p. 1). Finally, the connections section relates the performance expectations from a given standard to the CCSS, disciplinary core ideas at other grade levels, and other science disciplines at the same grade level.

Figure 1.3 (page 12) shows the first-grade standard related to the core idea of Heredity: Inheritance and Variation of Traits.

1-LS3   Heredity: Inheritance and Variation of Traits

Students who demonstrate understanding can:

1-LS3-1. Make observations to construct an evidence-based account that young plants and animals are like, but not exactly like, their parents.

[Clarification Statement: Examples of patterns could include features plants or animals share. Examples of observations could include leaves from the same kind of plant are the same shape but can differ in size; and, a particular breed of dog looks like its parents but is not exactly the same.]

[Assessment Boundary: Assessment does not include inheritance or animals that undergo metamorphosis or hybrids.]

The performance expectations above were developed using the following elements from the NRC document *A Framework for K–12 Science Education*:

Science and Engineering Practices	Disciplinary Core Ideas	Crosscutting Concepts
Constructing Explanations and Designing Solutions Constructing explanations and designing solutions in K–2 builds on prior experiences and progresses to the use of evidence and ideas in constructing evidence-based accounts of natural phenomena and designing solutions. • Make observations (firsthand or from media) to construct an evidence-based account for natural phenomena. (1-LS3-1)	**LS3.A: Inheritance of Traits** • Young animals are very much, but not exactly, like their parents. Plants also are very much, but not exactly, like their parents. (1-LS3-1) **LS3.B: Variation of Traits** • Individuals of the same kind of plant or animal are recognizable as similar but can also vary in many ways. (1-LS3-1)	**Patterns** • Patterns in the natural world can be observed, used to describe phenomena, and used as evidence. (1-LS3-1)

Connections to other DCIs in first grade: N/A

Articulation of DCIs across grade levels: 3.LS3.A (1-LS3-1); 3.LS3.B (1-LS3-1)

Common Core State Standards Connections:

ELA/Literacy–

RI.1.1	Ask and answer questions about key details in a text. (1-LS3-1)
W.1.7	Participate in shared research and writing projects (e.g., explore a number of "how-to" books on a given topic and use them to write a sequence of instructions). (1-LS3-1)
W.1.8	With guidance and support from adults, recall information from experiences or gather information from provided sources to answer a question. (1-LS3-1)

Mathematics–

MP.2	Reason abstractly and quantitatively. (1-LS3-1)
MP.5	Use appropriate tools strategically. (1-LS3-1)
1.MD.A.1	Order three objects by length; compare the lengths of two objects indirectly by using a third object. (1-LS3-1)

Source: Achieve, 2013a, p. 13.

Figure 1.3: Grade 1 NGSS standard for the core idea of Heredity: Inheritance and Variation of Traits.

The standard shown in figure 1.3 contains one performance expectation—"Students who demonstrate understanding can: Make observations to construct an evidence-based account that young plants and animals are like, but not exactly like, their parents" (Achieve, 2013a, p. 13). All the elements in the foundation boxes pertain to the single performance expectation.

Performance expectation codes appeared to the left of each performance expectation in the NGSS. Each code identified the grade level, discipline, core idea, and performance expectation number of the performance expectation associated with it. The grade level identifications were fairly straightforward. A number indicated the corresponding grade level (for example, 1 meant grade 1), and K, MS, and HS aligned to kindergarten, middle school, and high school, respectively.

The following letter combinations related a performance expectation to its specific discipline.

- ✦ Physical sciences = PS

- ✦ Life sciences = LS

- ✦ Earth and space sciences = ESS

- ✦ Engineering, technology, and applications of science = ETS

Although the NGSS named the fourth discipline *engineering, technology, and applications of science*, we simply refer to this discipline as *engineering*.

The number immediately following each discipline abbreviation signaled the core idea within a discipline with which a performance expectation was associated. A list of the core ideas within each discipline can be found in table 1.3 (page 9) or 1.4 (page 10). The final number at the end of a performance expectation code identified which performance expectation within a core idea the code referenced.

Thus, the performance expectation code found in figure 1.3 (1-LS3-1) indicates that the performance expectation is at the first-grade level. The LS3 relates this performance expectation to the core idea of Heredity: Inheritance and Variation of Traits within the discipline of life sciences. The 1 at the end of the performance expectation code identifies this specific performance expectation as the first performance expectation in its core idea of Heredity: Inheritance and Variation of Traits.

Performance expectation codes appeared in each of the foundation boxes to allow the reader "to see how the information in the foundation boxes is used to construct each performance expectation" (Achieve, 2013b, p. 3). The codes also served as a way to navigate the NGSS. As seen in figure 1.3, the connections section refers the reader to 3.LS3 to see the performance expectation in the standard articulated at a higher grade level.

Summary

In this chapter, we discussed the process used to create the NGSS and the organization and format of the standards themselves. The multiyear process for creating the NGSS included two parts: (1) conceptualization and (2) writing. The conceptualization process involved international benchmarking and the creation of the NRC framework, which informed the writing of the NGSS. Each NGSS performance expectation is built from elements of the three dimensions in the framework: (1) scientific and engineering practices, (2) crosscutting concepts, and (3) disciplinary core ideas. In the next chapter, we discuss how the proficiency scales found in part II (page 55) developed from the NGSS.

2

Measurement Topics, Proficiency Scales, and the NGSS

Even a cursory reading of chapter 1 demonstrates that the Next Generation Science Standards (NGSS; NGSS Lead States, 2013) were a remarkable accomplishment—both broad in scope yet deep in rigor. But these laudable characteristics also made them difficult for a busy teacher to implement. This book is intended to help teachers translate content from the NGSS into a format that guides both assessment and instruction through the use of proficiency scales.

The Nature of Proficiency Scales

In simple terms, a *proficiency scale* can be thought of as the organization of important content for a specific topic into three levels of difficulty: (1) the target content, (2) the simpler content, and (3) the more complex content. To illustrate, consider the following target content a middle school science teacher might identify as a goal:

> The student will analyze and interpret data on natural hazards to forecast future catastrophic events and inform the development of technologies to mitigate their effects.

This represents the desired level of knowledge the teacher would like all students to attain as the result of a specific lesson or set of lessons and is commonly referred to as the *target learning goal* or simply the *learning goal*. In this case, the target learning goal is taken directly from the NGSS (more specifically, from performance expectation MS-ESS3-2; see Achieve, 2013a, p. 72).

To create a proficiency scale, a teacher must also identify simpler content that is essential to students' understanding of the target learning goal. We refer to this as the *simpler learning goal*. This simpler but essential content is usually the subject of direct instruction. In this case, the teacher might identify the following as simpler but essential content:

The student will:

✦ Recognize or recall specific vocabulary (for example, *catastrophic, drought, earthquake, flood, forecast, frequency, hurricane, location, mitigate, natural hazard, predict, reservoir, satellite, severe weather, technology, tornado, tsunami, volcanic eruption*).

✦ Describe natural hazards.

✦ Describe indicators that a natural hazard may occur.

✦ Describe technologies that can mitigate the effects of natural hazards.

A teacher would also identify a *more complex learning goal*, which requires that students go above and beyond what has already been taught. In this case, the more complex content might be:

> The student will research a strategy in place to mitigate the effects of natural hazards, identify the strategy's shortcomings, and develop possible solutions that would address its weaknesses.

These three levels of learning goals—simpler, target, and more complex—represent a progression of understanding used to direct both instruction and assessment.

Once a teacher identifies three levels of learning goals, he or she can articulate a formal scale. The general format for a proficiency scale is depicted in table 2.1.

Table 2.1: Generic Proficiency Scale Format

Score 4.0	More complex learning goal	
	Score 3.5	*In addition to score 3.0 performance, partial success at score 4.0 content*
Score 3.0	Target learning goal	
	Score 2.5	*No major errors or omissions regarding score 2.0 content, and partial success at score 3.0 content*
Score 2.0	Simpler learning goal	
	Score 1.5	*Partial success at score 2.0 content, and major errors or omissions regarding score 3.0 content*
Score 1.0	With help, partial success at score 2.0 content and score 3.0 content	
	Score 0.5	*With help, partial success at score 2.0 content but not at score 3.0 content*
Score 0.0	Even with help, no success	

Source: Adapted from Marzano, 2009, p. 67.

By inserting simpler, target, and more complex goals into the generic scale found in table 2.1 as score 2.0, 3.0, and 4.0 content respectively, teachers can create topic-specific proficiency scales. For example, table 2.2 presents a proficiency scale created from the previously identified target, simpler, and more complex goals related to natural hazards.

As shown in table 2.2, the score 3.0 content—the target learning goal—is a performance expectation taken directly from the NGSS (MS-ESS3-2; see Achieve, 2013a, p. 72). In this particular example, only one performance expectation is referenced at the score 3.0 level of the proficiency scale. However, some proficiency scales in part II (page 55) include multiple performance expectations from the NGSS as score 3.0 elements. The score 2.0 content includes basic vocabulary and processes that relate to the element or elements of the target learning goal stated at the score 3.0 level. A score of 1.0 indicates that, when working independently, a student does not demonstrate proficiency with the score 2.0 and 3.0 content but demonstrates partial proficiency with the aid of a teacher. A score of 0.0 indicates that even with help, the student does not have success with the content. The proficiency scale also includes half-point scores (found at the score 0.5, 1.5, 2.5, and 3.5 level). Half-point scores indicate that a student has reached one level of proficiency but is still working toward the next learning goal.

Table 2.2: Middle School Proficiency Scale for Natural Hazards

Score 4.0	The student will:
	Research a strategy in place to mitigate the effects of natural hazards, identify the strategy's shortcomings, and develop possible solutions that would address its weaknesses.
	Score 3.5 — *In addition to score 3.0 performance, partial success at score 4.0 content*
Score 3.0	The student will:
	Analyze and interpret data on natural hazards to forecast future catastrophic events and inform the development of technologies to mitigate their effects.
	Score 2.5 — *No major errors or omissions regarding score 2.0 content, and partial success at score 3.0 content*
Score 2.0	The student will: • Recognize or recall specific vocabulary (for example, *catastrophic, drought, earthquake, flood, forecast, frequency, hurricane, location, mitigate, natural hazard, predict, reservoir, satellite, severe weather, technology, tornado, tsunami, volcanic eruption*). • Describe natural hazards. • Describe indicators that a natural hazard may occur. • Describe technologies that can mitigate the effects of natural hazards.
	Score 1.5 — *Partial success at score 2.0 content, and major errors or omissions regarding score 3.0 content*
Score 1.0	With help, partial success at score 2.0 content and score 3.0 content
	Score 0.5 — *With help, partial success at score 2.0 content but not at score 3.0 content*
Score 0.0	Even with help, no success

Proficiency Scales Organized Into Measurement Topics

The majority of this book contains proficiency scales derived from the NGSS. Researchers at Marzano Research analyzed the NGSS and constructed the scales as a tool to help educators implement the standards in a parsimonious fashion. During this process, the work group identified essential knowledge and skills found within the NGSS and created proficiency scales for that knowledge, eventually organizing the scales into measurement topics.

Measurement topics are the broad content categories into which proficiency scales are organized. As discussed in chapter 1, the NGSS were organized by four disciplines: (1) physical sciences, (2) life sciences, (3) Earth and space sciences, and (4) engineering, technology, and applications of science. Each discipline was divided into core ideas, which were themselves divided into sub-ideas. In all, the NGSS identified thirteen core ideas and forty-four sub-ideas (see table 1.4, page 10). For example, there are four core ideas within the discipline of physical sciences: (1) Matter and Its Interactions, (2) Motion and Stability: Forces and Interactions, (3) Energy, and (4) Waves and Their Applications in Technologies for Information Transfer. The core idea of Matter and Its Interactions has three sub-ideas.

The measurement topics presented in this book have a much simpler structure with only two levels. The top level consists of the four disciplines of science mentioned previously, which align with the disciplines from the NGSS. The second level contains forty-seven measurement topics: fifteen for physical sciences, fifteen for life sciences, fourteen for Earth and space sciences, and three for engineering. Measurement topics typically span more than one grade level. Thus, the measurement topics can be likened to the sub-ideas within the NGSS. Indeed, the measurement topics were strongly informed by, yet are not identical to, the sub-ideas found in the NGSS. Each measurement topic contains one or more proficiency scales, each at a specific grade level or grade-level band. Table 2.3 lists the forty-seven measurement topics within the four disciplines and identifies the grade levels for the proficiency scales that each measurement topic contains.

Table 2.3: Proficiency Scales by Measurement Topics and Grade Level

Measurement Topic	HS	MS	5	4	3	2	1	K
Physical Sciences								
Forces and Interactions	X	X		X	X			X
Electric and Magnetic Forces	X	X			X			
Gravity	X	X	X					
Energy and Forces	X	X						
Energy Definitions	X	X		X				
Energy Conservation and Energy Transfer	X	X		X				X
Waves	X	X		X			X	
Electromagnetic Radiation	X			X			X	
Information Technologies	X	X		X			X	
States of Matter		X				X		
Structure and Properties of Matter	X	X	X			X		
Conservation of Matter	X	X	X					
Chemical Reactions	X	X	X					
Bonds	X							
Nuclear Processes	X							
Life Sciences								
Growth and Development of Organisms		X			X		X	
Matter and Energy in Organisms	X	X	X			X		X
Ecosystem Dynamics	X	X				X		
Interdependent Relationships in Ecosystems	X	X			X	X		
Matter and Energy in Ecosystems	X	X	X					
Humans, Biodiversity, and Ecosystems	X	X						
Structure and Function	X	X		X			X	
Information Processing		X		X				
Cell Theory	X	X						
Inheritance of Traits	X	X			X		X	
Variation of Traits	X	X			X			
Adaptation	X	X			X			
Natural Selection	X	X			X			
Fossils		X			X			
Evidence of Common Ancestry	X	X						

Measurement Topic	HS	MS	5	4	3	2	1	K
Earth and Space Sciences								
The Solar System	X	X	X				X	
The Universe and Stars	X		X				X	
Weather and Climate	X	X			X			X
Natural Hazards		X		X	X			X
Weathering and Erosion				X		X		
Water and Earth's Surface	X	X	X			X		
Earth's History	X	X		X		X		
Plate Tectonics	X	X		X		X		
Earth Systems	X	X	X					
Humans and Earth Systems	X	X	X					X
Biogeology	X							X
Natural Resources	X	X		X				X
Global Climate Change	X	X						
Carbon Cycle	X							
Engineering								
Defining Problems	X	X	X			X		
Designing Solutions	X	X	X			X		
Evaluating and Testing Solutions	X	X	X			X		

Note: Engineering measurement topics are divided into grade-level ranges of K–2, 3–5, middle school, and high school.

The listing in table 2.3 constitutes an outline of K–12 science content that can be used by schools and districts to plan and implement NGSS-based instruction and assessment in an efficient and focused manner.

Defining Features of Proficiency Scales

Various unique features define the proficiency scales found in part II (page 55) of this book. As described previously, each scale includes three levels of content that represent the target learning goal (score 3.0 content), simpler learning goal (score 2.0 content), and more complex learning goal (score 4.0 content). Table 2.4 (page 20) shows a proficiency scale from part II of this book.

The proficiency scale depicted in table 2.4 contains one element at score 3.0:

> **4-ESS2-1—Make observations and/or measurements to provide evidence of the effects of weathering or the rate of erosion by water, ice, wind, or vegetation** (for example, observe or measure the amount of vegetation, speed of wind, relative rate of deposition, angle of slope in the downhill movement of water, cycles of freezing and thawing of water, cycles of heating and cooling, or volume of water flow to give evidence of the effects of weathering and the rate of erosion).

The bolded language present at the score 3.0 level of each proficiency scale is taken directly from the NGSS performance expectations. In this case, the score 3.0 element contains the performance expectation 4-ESS2-1 (see Achieve, 2013a, p. 35). The information in parentheses after each performance expectation summarizes its associated clarification statement found in the NGSS. The score 2.0 content

Table 2.4: Grade 4 Proficiency Scale for the Measurement Topic of Weathering and Erosion

Score 4.0	In addition to score 3.0 performance, the student demonstrates in-depth inferences and applications that go beyond what was taught.	
	Score 3.5	*In addition to score 3.0 performance, partial success at score 4.0 content*
Score 3.0	The student will: **4-ESS2-1—Make observations and/or measurements to provide evidence of the effects of weathering or the rate of erosion by water, ice, wind, or vegetation** (for example, observe or measure the amount of vegetation, speed of wind, relative rate of deposition, angle of slope in the downhill movement of water, cycles of freezing and thawing of water, cycles of heating and cooling, or volume of water flow to give evidence of the effects of weathering and the rate of erosion).	
	Score 2.5	*No major errors or omissions regarding score 2.0 content, and partial success at score 3.0 content*
Score 2.0	4-ESS2-1—The student will: • Recognize or recall specific vocabulary (for example, *angle, cool, cycle, deposition, downhill, erosion, erosion resistance, freeze, heat, ice, rate, relative, slope, soil erosion, speed, thaw, vegetation, volume, water, water flow, weathering, wind*). • Describe the effects of weathering or erosion by water, ice, wind, or vegetation.	
	Score 1.5	*Partial success at score 2.0 content, and major errors or omissions regarding score 3.0 content*
Score 1.0	With help, partial success at score 2.0 content and score 3.0 content	
	Score 0.5	*With help, partial success at score 2.0 content but not at score 3.0 content*
Score 0.0	Even with help, no success	

in each scale derives from the NGSS performance expectations, but the content is not explicitly stated as a performance expectation. Rather, an understanding of score 2.0 content is necessary to achieve score 3.0 status in a proficiency scale, but the understanding is implied—rather than explicit—in the performance expectation and its accompanying clarification statement. Typically, score 2.0 content contains vocabulary terms, factual information, and basic skills necessary to attain score 3.0 status. The vocabulary terms found at this level were pulled directly from respective score 3.0 elements, though some scales contain additional vocabulary terms from the book *Building Background Knowledge for Academic Achievement* (Marzano, 2004) when appropriate. Finally, the score 4.0 content in table 2.4 contains the following generalized statement for a learning goal more complex than the score 3.0 content: "In addition to score 3.0 performance, the student demonstrates in-depth inferences and applications that go beyond what was taught." (We discuss how to generate more specific score 4.0 learning goals starting on page 24 in a subsequent section of this chapter.)

Some proficiency scales include multiple elements at the score 3.0 level. For example, unlike the proficiency scale in table 2.4, the proficiency scale in table 2.5 has two elements in the score 3.0 section and two corresponding elements in the score 2.0 section. Performance expectation codes relate the score 3.0 elements taken directly from the NGSS performance expectations to the score 2.0 elements implied in the performance expectations.

The two performance expectations included together as score 3.0 content in the proficiency scale in table 2.5 are highly related and could easily be taught together. Specifically, they both pertain to the cycle of Earth's materials (fossils and rocks) through and within the Earth's crust (continental shapes and seafloor structures). These two performance expectations were also listed together in the NGSS within the discipline of Earth and space sciences under the core idea of Earth's Systems (see Achieve, 2013a, p.

Table 2.5: Middle School Proficiency Scale for the Measurement Topic of Plate Tectonics

Score 4.0	In addition to score 3.0 performance, the student demonstrates in-depth inferences and applications that go beyond what was taught.	
	Score 3.5	*In addition to score 3.0 performance, partial success at score 4.0 content*
Score 3.0	The student will: **MS-ESS2-1—Develop a model to describe the cycling of Earth's materials and the flow of energy that drives this process** (for example, create and use a model to explain the processes of melting, crystallization, weathering, deformation, and sedimentation, which act together to form minerals and rocks through the cycling of Earth's materials). **MS-ESS2-3—Analyze and interpret data on the distribution of fossils and rocks, continental shapes, and seafloor structures to provide evidence of the past plate motions** (for example, analyze and interpret the similarities of rock and fossil types on different continents; the shapes of the continents, including continental shelves; and the locations of seafloor structures, such as ridges, fracture zones, and trenches to give evidence of past plate motions).	
	Score 2.5	*No major errors or omissions regarding score 2.0 content, and partial success at score 3.0 content*
Score 2.0	**MS-ESS2-1**—The student will: • Recognize or recall specific vocabulary (for example, *crystal, crystalline solid, crystallization, cycle, deformation, Earth material, energy, flow, formation, melt, mineral, recrystallization, sedimentation, weathering*). • Describe the role of melting, crystallization, weathering, deformation, and sedimentation in the formation of rocks and minerals. **MS-ESS2-3**—The student will: • Recognize or recall specific vocabulary (for example, *continent, continental shape, continental shelf, distribution, Earth's crust, fossil, fracture zone, geologic force, geologic shift, lithosphere, motion, plate, ridge, rock layer movement, seafloor structure, trench*). • Describe ways in which the Earth's surface has changed over time. • Describe how distribution of fossils, rocks, continental shapes, and seafloor structures give evidence of past plate motions.	
	Score 1.5	*Partial success at score 2.0 content, and major errors or omissions regarding score 3.0 content*
Score 1.0	With help, partial success at score 2.0 content and score 3.0 content	
	Score 0.5	*With help, partial success at score 2.0 content but not at score 3.0 content*
Score 0.0	Even with help, no success	

70). Thus, with a direct relationship established, the two elements appear together in a proficiency scale for the measurement topic of Plate Tectonics.

As another example of two elements in a single proficiency scale, consider the high school proficiency scale for the measurement topic of Humans, Biodiversity, and Ecosystems (page 89). The score 3.0 section of the proficiency scale contains the following two elements (two performance expectations pulled directly from the NGSS).

1. **HS-LS2-7—Design, evaluate, and refine a solution for reducing the impacts of human activities on the environment and biodiversity** (for example, use scientific knowledge, student-generated sources of evidence, prioritized criteria, and tradeoff considerations to design, evaluate, and refine a solution for reducing the environmental impact of human activities such as urbanization, construction of dams, and dissemination of invasive species).

2. **HS-LS4-6—Create or revise a simulation to test a solution to mitigate adverse impacts of human activity on biodiversity** (for example, design a solution for a proposed problem related to threatened or endangered species or to genetic variation of organisms for multiple species, and create and revise a simulation to test that solution).

This measurement topic concerns itself with the impact human activity has on the environment, and more specifically, the negative effect of human activity on biodiversity. Again, the two performance expectations overlap: a student who creates a simulation to test a solution to mitigate adverse impacts of human activity on biodiversity (HS-LS4-6; see Achieve, 2013a, p. 95) may begin by designing a solution that reduces the impacts of human activities on the environment and biodiversity (thus addressing the performance expectation HS-LS2-7; see Achieve, 2013a, p. 92). In the NGSS, the two performance expectations are found in different core ideas. HS-LS4-6 can be found within the core idea of Biological Evolution: Unity and Diversity, whereas HS-LS2-7 falls within the core idea of Ecosystems: Interactions, Energy, and Dynamics. However, our analysis determined these related elements could be grouped together within one proficiency scale for the measurement topic of Humans, Biodiversity, and Ecosystems.

Table 2.6 lists the number of performance expectations from the NGSS found in each proficiency scale at each grade level of a measurement topic. When reading this table, it is important to note that there is only one proficiency scale per measurement topic at each grade level. Cells containing an *N/A* indicate that a grade level does not have a proficiency scale related to that specific measurement topic.

Table 2.6: Number of Performance Expectations per Measurement Topic per Grade Level

Measurement Topic	HS	MS	5	4	3	2	1	K	Total
Physical Sciences									
Forces and Interactions	3	2	N/A	1	2	N/A	N/A	2	10
Electric and Magnetic Forces	2	2	N/A	N/A	2	N/A	N/A	N/A	6
Gravity	1	1	1	N/A	N/A	N/A	N/A	N/A	3
Energy and Forces	1	1	N/A	N/A	N/A	N/A	N/A	N/A	2
Energy Definitions	3	1	N/A	1	N/A	N/A	N/A	N/A	5
Energy Conservation and Energy Transfer	1	3	N/A	2	N/A	N/A	N/A	2	8
Waves	1	2	N/A	1	N/A	N/A	1	N/A	5
Electromagnetic Radiation	2	N/A	N/A	1	N/A	N/A	2	N/A	5
Information Technologies	2	1	N/A	1	N/A	N/A	1	N/A	5
States of Matter	N/A	1	N/A	N/A	N/A	1	N/A	N/A	2
Structure and Properties of Matter	3	1	2	N/A	N/A	3	N/A	N/A	9
Conservation of Matter	1	1	1	N/A	N/A	N/A	N/A	N/A	3
Chemical Reactions	3	3	1	N/A	N/A	N/A	N/A	N/A	7
Bonds	1	N/A	N/A	N/A	N/A	N/A	N/A	N/A	1
Nuclear Processes	1	N/A	N/A	N/A	N/A	N/A	N/A	N/A	1
Total	25	19	5	7	4	4	4	4	72
Life Sciences									
Growth and Development of Organisms	N/A	2	N/A	N/A	1	N/A	1	N/A	4

Measurement Topic	HS	MS	5	4	3	2	1	K	Total
Matter and Energy in Organisms	3	2	2	N/A	N/A	1	N/A	1	9
Ecosystem Dynamics	3	2	N/A	N/A	N/A	1	N/A	N/A	6
Interdependent Relationships in Ecosystems	1	1	N/A	N/A	1	1	N/A	N/A	4
Matter and Energy in Ecosystems	3	1	1	N/A	N/A	N/A	N/A	N/A	5
Humans, Biodiversity, and Ecosystems	2	1	N/A	N/A	N/A	N/A	N/A	N/A	3
Structure and Function	2	1	N/A	1	N/A	N/A	1	N/A	5
Information Processing	N/A	1	N/A	1	N/A	N/A	N/A	N/A	2
Cell Theory	2	2	N/A	N/A	N/A	N/A	N/A	N/A	4
Inheritance of Traits	1	1	N/A	N/A	1	N/A	1	N/A	4
Variation of Traits	2	1	N/A	N/A	1	N/A	N/A	N/A	4
Adaptation	2	1	N/A	N/A	2	N/A	N/A	N/A	5
Natural Selection	2	2	N/A	N/A	1	N/A	N/A	N/A	5
Fossils	N/A	1	N/A	N/A	1	N/A	N/A	N/A	2
Evidence of Common Ancestry	1	2	N/A	N/A	N/A	N/A	N/A	N/A	3
Total	24	21	3	2	8	3	3	1	65
Earth and Space Sciences									
The Solar System	1	3	1	N/A	N/A	N/A	1	N/A	6
The Universe and Stars	3	N/A	1	N/A	N/A	N/A	1	N/A	5
Weather and Climate	1	2	N/A	N/A	2	N/A	N/A	1	6
Natural Hazards	N/A	1	N/A	1	1	N/A	N/A	1	4
Weathering and Erosion	N/A	N/A	N/A	1	N/A	1	N/A	N/A	2
Water and Earth's Surface	1	1	1	N/A	N/A	1	N/A	N/A	4
Earth's History	1	1	N/A	1	N/A	1	N/A	N/A	4
Plate Tectonics	2	2	N/A	1	N/A	1	N/A	N/A	6
Earth Systems	2	1	1	N/A	N/A	N/A	N/A	N/A	4
Humans and Earth Systems	2	1	1	N/A	N/A	N/A	N/A	1	5
Biogeology	1	N/A	N/A	N/A	N/A	N/A	N/A	1	2
Natural Resources	2	2	N/A	1	N/A	N/A	N/A	1	6
Global Climate Change	2	1	N/A	N/A	N/A	N/A	N/A	N/A	3
Carbon Cycle	1	N/A	N/A	N/A	N/A	N/A	N/A	N/A	1
Total	19	15	5	5	3	4	2	5	58
Total Performance Expectations	**68**	**55**	**13**	**14**	**15**	**11**	**9**	**10**	**195**
Engineering									
Defining Problems	1	1	1			1			4
Designing Solutions	1	1	1			1			4
Evaluating and Testing Solutions	2	2	1			1			6
Total	4	4	3			3			14

Note: Engineering measurement topics are divided into grade-level ranges of K–2, 3–5, middle school, and high school.

As table 2.6 shows, each individual proficiency scale contains no more than three performance expectations. However, the vast majority of measurement topics have only one performance expectation from the NGSS. Specifically, of the 147 proficiency scales embedded in the forty-seven measurement topics across grades K–12, ninety-seven (66.0%) include only one performance expectation, thirty-eight (25.8%) have two performance expectations, and only twelve (8.2%) have three performance expectations. This noted, if a school or district wished to create separate proficiency scales for a scale that contains more than one performance expectation, it could easily do so.

The proficiency scales, as currently articulated, represent a fairly tight curriculum. Each grade level has specific proficiency scales, and from grade level to grade level, the scales are organized into measurement topics that constitute a vertically connected science curriculum. Table 2.7 depicts the distribution of proficiency scales by grade level.

Table 2.7: Number of Proficiency Scales by Grade Level and Discipline

Grade Level	Physical Sciences	Life Sciences	Earth and Space Sciences	Engineering	Total
K	2	1	5	N/A	8
1	3	3	2		8
2	2	3	4		9
K–2	N/A	N/A	N/A	3	3
3	2	7	2	N/A	11
4	6	2	5		13
5	4	2	5		11
3–5	N/A	N/A	N/A	3	3
MS	12	15	10	3	40
HS	14	12	12	3	41
Total	45	45	45	12	147

Note: Engineering measurement topics are divided into grade-level ranges of K–2, 3–5, middle school, and high school.

As shown in table 2.7, no grade level has an inordinate number of proficiency scales. Grade 4 has thirteen proficiency scales, not counting the engineering scales, and sixteen counting them—certainly a reasonable number of scales to implement across a 180-day school year. Middle school has forty proficiency scales, but they are spread out over three grade levels (grades 6–8), and high school has forty-one proficiency scales spread across four grade levels (grades 9–12). In effect, the proficiency scales make the task of teaching the performance expectations articulated in the NGSS a rather straightforward process.

Developing More Complex (Score 4.0) Learning Goals

The scales presented in part II (page 55) of this book do not include content-specific score 4.0 learning goals. Rather, the score 4.0 section of each proficiency scale reads, "In addition to score 3.0 performance, the student demonstrates in-depth inferences and applications that go beyond what was taught." We use this convention because many of the schools and districts we have worked with prefer to establish their own local score 4.0 learning goals. To create learning goals at this level, we recommend using one of the many taxonomies that are available, such as Norman L. Webb's (2006) or Lorin W. Anderson and David R. Krathwohl's (2001). Here we use Robert J. Marzano and John S. Kendall's (2007) New Taxonomy, which is shown in table 2.8.

Table 2.8: Level of Difficulty of Mental Processes in Marzano and Kendall's (2007) New Taxonomy

Level of Difficulty	Mental Processes
Level 4: Knowledge Utilization	Decision Making Problem Solving Experimenting Investigating
Level 3: Analysis	Matching Classifying Analyzing Errors Generalizing Specifying
Level 2: Comprehension	Integrating Symbolizing
Level 1: Retrieval	Executing Recalling Recognizing

Source: Marzano, 2009, p. 28.

Score 4.0 learning goals typically fall at level 3 (analysis) or level 4 (knowledge utilization) difficulty of the taxonomy. Specific terms and phrases associated with these two levels of difficulty can be useful when designing score 4.0 learning goals. Table 2.9 (pages 26–28) lists some of these terms as well as terms and phrases for lower levels of the taxonomy.

To construct a score 4.0 learning goal for a proficiency scale, one must first identify the difficulty level of the content articulated as the score 3.0 learning goal. For example, the score 3.0 learning goal in the proficiency scale in table 2.2 (page 17) states that a student will "analyze and interpret data on natural hazards to forecast future catastrophic events and inform the development of technologies to mitigate their effects." A teacher might focus on the word *forecast* as a key term and recognize that it is a synonym for *predict*. In table 2.9, *predict* is shown as an identifying term for the mental process of specifying, which indicates a level 3 (analysis) difficulty on the taxonomy. A teacher might also identify the terms *analyze* and *interpret* as further evidence to confirm that the target learning goal falls at level 3 difficulty.

With the difficulty level of the score 3.0 learning goal serving as a reference point, the teacher might decide to write the score 4.0 content one difficulty level higher at level 4 (knowledge utilization) of the taxonomy. Specifically, the teacher might wish for students to engage in the mental process of investigating—found at level 4 difficulty—to demonstrate proficiency with score 4.0 content. One of the verbs associated with investigating is *research*. Using this as a prompt, a teacher might write the following score 4.0 learning goal:

> The student will research a strategy in place to mitigate the effects of natural hazards, identify the strategy's shortcomings, and develop possible solutions that would address its weaknesses.

Table 2.2 (page 17) depicts these learning goals integrated into the proficiency scale format.

This section briefly introduced the concept of generating complex score 4.0 learning goals and provided tables 2.8 and 2.9 as tools to generate such goals. A more detailed description of the New Taxonomy is presented in appendix A (page 127).

Table 2.9: Level of Difficulty and Terms and Phrases Associated With Mental Processes

Level of Difficulty	Mental Process	Terms and Phrases
Level 4 Knowledge Utilization	Decision Making	Decide Select the best among the following alternatives Which among the following would be the best What is the best way Which of these is most suitable
	Problem Solving	Solve How would you overcome Adapt Develop a strategy to Figure out a way to How will you reach your goal under these conditions
	Experimenting	Experiment Generate and test Test the idea that What would happen if How would you test that How would you determine if How can this be explained Based on the experiment, what can be predicted
	Investigating	Investigate Research Find out about Take a position on What are the differing features of How did this happen Why did this happen What would have happened if

Level 3 Analysis	Matching	Categorize
		Compare and contrast
		Differentiate
		Discriminate
		Distinguish
		Sort
		Create an analogy
		Create a metaphor
	Classifying	Classify
		Organize
		Sort
		Identify a broader category
		Identify categories
		Identify different types
	Analyzing Errors	Identify errors
		Identify problems
		Identify issues
		Identify misunderstandings
		Assess
		Critique
		Diagnose
		Evaluate
		Edit
		Revise
	Generalizing	Generalize
		What conclusions can be drawn
		What inferences can be made
		Create a generalization
		Create a principle
		Create a rule
		Trace the development of
		Form conclusions
	Specifying	Make and defend
		Predict
		Judge
		Deduce
		What would have to happen
		Develop an argument for
		Under what conditions

continued ➤

Level 2 Comprehension	Integrating	Describe how or why
		Describe the key parts of
		Describe the effects
		Describe the relationship between
		Explain ways in which
		Paraphrase
		Summarize
	Symbolizing	Symbolize
		Depict
		Represent
		Illustrate
		Draw
		Show
		Use models
		Diagram
		Chart
Level 1 Retrieval	Recognizing	Recognize (from a list)
		Select from (a list)
		Identify (from a list)
		Determine (if the following statements are true)
	Recalling	Exemplify
		Name
		List
		Label
		State
		Describe
		Identify who
		Describe what
		Identify where
		Identify when
	Executing	Use
		Demonstrate
		Show
		Make
		Complete
		Draft

Source: Marzano, 2009, pp. 124–126.

Summary

This chapter introduced the idea of proficiency scales and explained the system of organization—measurement topics—used to present the proficiency scales in this book. The chapter elaborated on the connection between the proficiency scales in part II (page 55) and the NGSS—how the NGSS informed the creation of each proficiency scale as well as how the organization of the NGSS influenced the organization of the proficiency scales into measurement topics. Finally, this chapter explored the three types of content learning goals that compose a proficiency scale and described how educators can use a taxonomy to create score 4.0 learning goals. The next chapter explains how proficiency scales can inform instruction.

3

Proficiency Scales and Classroom Instruction

Effective instruction begins with effective planning, and use of a proficiency scale often optimizes the planning process. To illustrate, assume that a middle school teacher is planning instruction for a set of lessons on the measurement topic of Water and Earth's Surface using the proficiency scale shown in table 3.1.

Table 3.1: Middle School Proficiency Scale for the Measurement Topic of Water and Earth's Surface

	Middle School	
Score 4.0	In addition to score 3.0 performance, the student demonstrates in-depth inferences and applications that go beyond what was taught.	
	Score 3.5	*In addition to score 3.0 performance, partial success at score 4.0 content*
Score 3.0	The student will: **MS-ESS2-4—Develop a model to describe the cycling of water through Earth's systems driven by energy from the sun and the force of gravity** (for example, create a conceptual or physical model to explain how water changes state as it moves through the multiple pathways of the hydrologic cycle).	
	Score 2.5	*No major errors or omissions regarding score 2.0 content, and partial success at score 3.0 content*
Score 2.0	**MS-ESS2-4**—The student will: • Recognize or recall specific vocabulary (for example, *cycle, Earth system, energy, force, gravity, hydrologic cycle, percolation, water cycle*). • Describe each phase of the hydrologic cycle.	
	Score 1.5	*Partial success at score 2.0 content, and major errors or omissions regarding score 3.0 content*
Score 1.0	With help, partial success at score 2.0 content and score 3.0 content	
	Score 0.5	*With help, partial success at score 2.0 content but not at score 3.0 content*
Score 0.0	Even with help, no success	

The proficiency scale in table 3.1 is from part II of this book (page 55). As described in chapter 2, the score 3.0 content for each proficiency scale in part II was taken directly from the Next Generation Science Standards' (NGSS; NGSS Lead States, 2013) performance expectations (though we paraphrased the associated clarification statements in parentheses). Researchers then used the score 3.0 content to inform the score 2.0 content. For planning purposes, however, a teacher might want to augment the scales with additional content. In fact, we strongly recommend that teachers add content or change the language of proficiency scales to tailor them to their own needs. With this in mind, teachers might add the following.

Additional Score 3.0 Content

The student will:

+ Explain how energy from the sun powers other Earth processes.

+ Explain how the force of gravity affects the Earth.

+ Explain various pathways of the hydrologic cycle.

Additional Score 2.0 Content

The student will:

+ Identify and define various Earth systems.

+ Describe the role of water in one of Earth's systems.

+ List different states of water and identify the relationships between them.

The teacher might also wish to articulate a more specific description of the score 4.0 learning goal. Using the process found in chapter 2, the teacher would first try to determine the taxonomy level of the score 3.0 content of the proficiency scale by consulting tables 2.8 and 2.9 (pages 25–28) as well as the descriptions of the taxonomy levels found in appendix A (page 127). The teacher might conclude that the score 3.0 content represents the process of symbolizing, which is found at level 2 (comprehension) difficulty of the taxonomy. Specifically, at level 2 difficulty, a student understands the overall structure of a topic—the critical versus noncritical elements and how they interact. In this case, the student must understand the critical versus noncritical aspects of how water cycles through Earth's systems and how energy from the sun and the force of gravity drive this cycle. The score 3.0 learning goal represents a symbolizing goal because students are required to translate their understanding into a model (or a pictographic representation) of the process of water cycling through the Earth's systems.

Knowing that the score 3.0 content in the proficiency scale is at level 2 (comprehension) difficulty of the taxonomy, the teacher decides to write the score 4.0 content at level 3 (analysis) difficulty of the taxonomy. Specifically, the teacher decides to create an error-analysis task. As described in appendix A, the process of error analysis involves identifying misconceptions or errors in thinking regarding a specific topic. For this topic, the teacher might write the following score 4.0 goal.

> The student will describe previous errors or misconceptions about the cycling of water through the Earth's systems.

With the new score 4.0 learning goal and the additional content for the score 2.0 and 3.0 learning goals articulated, the teacher might revise the proficiency scale as depicted in table 3.2.

The teacher-revised proficiency scale in table 3.2 provides more explicit direction for both instruction and assessment. In general, individual teachers should feel free to add content to the proficiency scales from part II of this book (page 55) to enhance the specificity of their instruction and assessment.

Table 3.2: Teacher-Revised Middle School Proficiency Scale for the Measurement Topic of Water and Earth's Surface

	Middle School	
Score 4.0	The student will:	
	MS-ESS2-4—Describe previous errors or misconceptions about the cycling of water through the Earth's systems.	
	Score 3.5	*In addition to score 3.0 performance, partial success at score 4.0 content*
Score 3.0	MS-ESS2-4—The student will:	
	• **Develop a model to describe the cycling of water through Earth's systems driven by energy from the sun and the force of gravity** (for example, create a conceptual or physical model to explain how water changes state as it moves through the multiple pathways of the hydrologic cycle).	
	• Explain how energy from the sun powers other Earth processes.	
	• Explain how the force of gravity affects the Earth.	
	• Describe various pathways of the hydrologic cycle.	
	Score 2.5	*No major errors or omissions regarding score 2.0 content, and partial success at score 3.0 content*
Score 2.0	MS-ESS2-4—The student will:	
	• Recognize or recall specific vocabulary (for example, *cycle, Earth system, energy, force, gravity, hydrologic cycle, percolation, water cycle*).	
	• Describe each phase of the hydrologic cycle.	
	• Identify and define various Earth systems.	
	• Describe the role of water in one of Earth's systems.	
	• List different states of water and identify the relationships between them.	
	Score 1.5	*Partial success at score 2.0 content, and major errors or omissions regarding score 3.0 content*
Score 1.0	With help, partial success at score 2.0 content and score 3.0 content	
	Score 0.5	*With help, partial success at score 2.0 content but not at score 3.0 content*
Score 0.0	Even with help, no success	

Three Types of Lessons

A proficiency scale designed for planning purposes should clearly define the topic of instruction as well as the various levels of difficulty of the content. While planning, a teacher should consider three types of lessons: (1) direct instruction lessons, (2) practicing and deepening lessons, and (3) knowledge application lessons.

Direct Instruction Lessons

As its name implies, a teacher explicitly presents content—most often new content—during a direct instruction lesson. These lessons operate under the assumption that when students are unfamiliar with content, the content should be taught directly. Often, content related to the simpler learning goal at the score 2.0 level of a proficiency scale is the subject of direct instruction lessons. To illustrate, the science teacher who created the scale in table 3.2 would probably plan one or more direct instruction lessons concerning factual information or details about the hydrologic cycle, Earth's systems, the role of water in Earth's systems, or states of water. Because score 2.0 content also includes vocabulary, the teacher would also directly define terms like *percolation* or explain the various phases that compose the water cycle.

Instructional strategies typically used during direct instruction lessons commonly include those in table 3.3.

Table 3.3: Strategies Used in Direct Instruction Lessons

Strategy	Description
Chunking Content	A teacher breaks down content into smaller segments of information so that it can be more easily understood by students. Specific strategies include presenting content in small chunks, using preassessment data to vary the size of each chunk, and chunk processing.
Processing Content	A teacher pauses during content presentation to help students actively process any new material. Specific strategies include perspective analysis, collaborative processing, and reciprocal teaching.
Recording and Representing Content	A teacher implements activities in the classroom that require students to record their understanding of new content visually or linguistically. Specific strategies include informal outlining, graphic organizers, and dramatic enactments.

Practicing and Deepening Lessons

Practicing and deepening lessons are designed to help students understand content at a more rigorous level and use skills, strategies, and processes more fluently and accurately. For example, once the science teacher has introduced the topic of the water cycle, he or she might engage students in a comparison task, such as creating a metaphor matrix like the one shown in table 3.4.

Table 3.4: Metaphor Matrix Comparing the Water Cycle to Paper Recycling

Term: Water Cycle	General Descriptors	Term: Paper Recycling
Cycles water through Earth's systems	Consists of a cycle that repeats over and over	Cycles paper through the human consumption system
Moves water between the atmosphere, the Earth's surface, and below the Earth's surface	Transports a substance to different locations	Moves paper between a consumer, a merchant, and various processing factories
Has multiple forks at each step in the cycle that create different pathways	Contains multiple pathways	Has multiple forks at each step in the cycle that create different pathways
Produces and maintains a supply of fresh water	Maintains a finite resource	Preserves trees by reducing the need for more to be cut down
Creates clean water through the evaporation and precipitation of groundwater	Creates a purification process	Creates new paper through the reduction of old paper products into paper pulp, which is later set into new paper

Instructional strategies commonly used during practicing and deepening lessons include those found in table 3.5.

Table 3.5: Strategies Used in Practicing and Deepening Lessons

Strategy	Description
Structured Practice Sessions	A teacher helps students develop fluency by engaging them in practice activities for content requiring a skill, strategy, or process. Specific strategies include modeling, guided practice, and varied practice.
Examining Similarities and Differences	A teacher helps students deepen their knowledge by asking them to examine similarities and differences between informational content. Specific strategies include Venn diagrams, comparison matrices, and sentence stem comparisons.
Examining Errors in Reasoning	A teacher helps students deepen their knowledge by asking them to examine their own reasoning or logic about informational content. Specific strategies include identifying errors of faulty logic, attack, weak reference, or misinformation; examining support for claims; and practicing identifying errors in logic.

Knowledge Application Lessons

Knowledge application lessons require students to go beyond what has been taught to generate new ideas about content. Knowledge application tasks are commonly derived directly from the score 4.0 content in a scale. In this case, the score 4.0 learning goal involves students describing previous errors or misconceptions about the cycling of water through Earth's systems. The knowledge application lessons for this unit would directly address how students would be expected to carry out this task. Knowledge application lessons usually involve the strategies depicted in table 3.6.

Table 3.6: Strategies Used in Knowledge Application Lessons

Strategy	Description
Engaging Students in Cognitively Complex Tasks	A teacher engages students in tasks that require decision making, problem solving, experimental inquiry, or investigation. Specific strategies include experimental-inquiry tasks, problem-solving tasks, and decision-making tasks.
Providing Resources and Guidance	A teacher guides students through cognitively complex tasks by providing resources and aid. Specific strategies include giving feedback, collecting assessment information, and providing scoring scales.
Having Students Generate and Defend Claims	A teacher asks students to make claims and use logical arguments to defend them. Specific strategies include generating claims, providing grounds, and providing backing.

Multiple Types of Lessons in One Class Period

It is important to note that a single class period might involve more than one lesson type. In fact, class periods often begin with a brief practicing and deepening lesson to sharpen students' understanding of previously presented content followed by a direct instruction lesson designed to introduce new knowledge. For example, a science teacher might begin a particular class period by presenting students with a comparison activity designed to deepen students' understanding of the different states of water. Next, the teacher would move to a direct instruction lesson designed to introduce new information about the characteristics of the different water states.

Instructional Strategies That Commonly Appear During All Types of Lessons

In addition to the instructional strategies specific to the three primary types of lessons, there are a number of strategies that can appear in any type of lesson. They include the strategies found in table 3.7.

Table 3.7: Strategies That Appear in All Types of Lessons

Strategy	Description
Previewing New Content	A teacher facilitates students linking what they already know to the content that is currently being addressed in class. Specific strategies include overt linkages, preview questions, and brief teacher summaries.
Highlighting Critical Information	A teacher alerts students to the crucial information within a lesson to which they should pay particular attention. Specific strategies include repetition of the most important content, visual and narrative activities, and pause time.
Elaborating on Content	A teacher asks students to make inferences about content that were not explicitly stated. Specific strategies include questioning sequences, general inferential questions, and elaborative interrogation.
Reviewing Content	A teacher reviews the critical information of a lesson with students to highlight specific content. Specific strategies include cumulative reviews, summaries, and demonstrations.
Revising Knowledge	A teacher asks students to revise their previous knowledge about content after the content has been addressed in a specific lesson. Specific strategies include peer feedback, academic notebook entries and reviews, and assignment revision.
Reflecting on Learning	A teacher engages students in a process of reflection regarding their learning and the learning process itself. Specific strategies include reflective journals, think logs, and exit slips.
Purposeful Homework	A teacher uses well-designed homework as a tool to deepen students' knowledge of content. Specific strategies include previewing homework, homework that deepens knowledge or practices a process or skill, and parent-assisted homework.
Organizing Students to Interact	A teacher uses small groups to organize students in order to facilitate the processing of new information. Specific strategies include grouping for active processing, fishbowl demonstrations, and grouping students using preassessment information.

For example, during any type of lesson, a teacher might alert students to pay particular attention to important content as it is addressed (highlighting critical information). Similarly, during any type of lesson, a teacher might stop and ask students to revise existing entries in their science notebooks to reflect their current level of understanding (revising knowledge).

Strategies That Set an Effective Context for Learning

In addition to the instructional strategies described earlier, there are a number of strategies that are important to establishing a context for learning. It is useful to remind oneself of these important strategies, even though they are commonly used and generic to most teaching situations. There are four categories of strategies that help set an effective context for learning: (1) engagement, (2) rules and procedures, (3) relationships, and (4) communicating high expectations.

As their name implies, engagement strategies capture and maintain students' attention. Rules and procedures provide a sense of safety and order in the classroom; strategies to this end articulate the standard operating procedures employed within a classroom. Relationship strategies help students feel accepted by both their teacher and their peers. Finally, strategies for communicating high expectations focus on reluctant learners and ensure that their voices are heard and respected in class. Appendix B (page 135) lists specific instructional strategies for each of these four areas, which, when used together, create an effective context for learning.

Planning for Daily Lessons

Thinking in terms of the score 2.0, 3.0, and 4.0 content in a proficiency scale, as well as the type of lessons to be used in class each day, provides the "big picture" in terms of how a set of lessons will unfold. To this end, a teacher might draft a rough unit plan identifying when to use direct instruction, practicing and deepening, and knowledge application lessons. In addition to a broad outline, a teacher might ask himself or herself specific questions that drive the design of daily lessons. To this end, we recommend the form depicted in figure 3.1 (page 38). Visit **marzanoresearch.com/reproducibles** for a blank reproducible of figure 3.1.

The form in figure 3.1 contains questions that cue a teacher to consider how the following elements can be integrated into a lesson plan:

+ The proficiency scale and the specific focus for the class period

+ The type of lessons to be employed in class

+ General instructional strategies that fit into any type of lesson the teacher will use in class

+ Engagement strategies the teacher will use in class

+ The strategies for rules and procedures, establishing relationships, and communicating high expectations the teacher will use in class

There is one section of the lesson plan in figure 3.1 that has not been mentioned yet: planning for assessments. This is addressed directly in the next chapter.

Teaching the Scientific and Engineering Practices

As described in chapter 1, *A Framework for K–12 Science Education: Practices, Crosscutting Concepts, and Core Ideas* (NRC, 2012) included three major dimensions: (1) scientific and engineering practices, (2) crosscutting concepts, and (3) disciplinary core ideas. The final format of the NGSS included all three dimensions in the context of the foundation boxes found in each standard (see figure 1.2, page 11). These three dimensions formed the basis for the construction of each of the NGSS performance expectations. Theoretically, each NGSS performance expectation integrates components of each of the three dimensions. Since the proficiency scales presented in this book are based on the NGSS performance expectations, a reasonable assumption would be that all three framework dimensions are inherent in the proficiency scales.

What will I do to remind students about the proficiency scale and the specific learning goals we will address today?

What type(s) of lessons will I use in today's class (direct instruction, practicing and deepening, knowledge application)?

What general instructional strategies will I use today?

How will I assess students during the class period?
- Whole-class assessment
- Individual student assessment

What activities will I use to ensure high engagement?

Are there specific students in class to whom I should pay particular attention, and what actions will I take with those students?
- Remind them of rules and procedures
- Actively establish positive relationships
- Actively communicate high expectations

Figure 3.1: Form for daily lesson planning.

However, one of the dimensions requires focused instruction over and above that required for the score 2.0, 3.0, and 4.0 content within a proficiency scale. Specifically, anytime students are expected to employ scientific and engineering practices, some direct instruction is most likely necessary. Recall from chapter 1 that there are eight such practices.

1. Asking questions and defining problems

2. Developing and using models

3. Planning and carrying out investigations

4. Analyzing and interpreting data

5. Using mathematics and computational thinking

6. Constructing explanations and designing solutions

7. Engaging in argument from evidence

8. Obtaining, evaluating, and communicating information

Each of these practices represents a relatively complex cognitive process that frequently shows up as score 4.0 content and sometimes as score 3.0 content in a proficiency scale. Because of the complexity of these practices, they should be taught directly to students. To illustrate, consider the process of engaging in argument from evidence. As noted by Katie Rogers and Julia A. Simms (2015), to engage in this process, teachers should provide students with a structure for an effective argument, such as the one in table 3.8.

Table 3.8: Four Elements of an Argument

Element	Definition	Example
Claim	A new idea or opinion. A claim may simply present information or suggest that certain action is needed.	Students should attend school year-round.
Grounds	The initial evidence—or reasoning—for a claim. Grounds are answers to the question, "Why do you think your claim is true?"	Over the summer, students forget what they learned in school.
Backing	Information or facts about grounds that help establish their validity. In some cases, backing is simply a more in-depth discussion of the grounds.	Alexander, Entwisle, and Olson (2007) found that during the school year, the academic growth of low-income students was comparable to that of other students. They reported that gaps in achievement actually occurred over the summer.
Qualifiers	Exceptions to claims that indicate the degree of certainty for the claim.	Year-round schooling may not be the only solution to this opportunity deficit for low-income students.

Source: Rogers & Simms, 2015, p. 18.

In addition to the four elements of an effective argument listed in table 3.8, teachers should also present students with signal words and phrases, such as those in table 3.9 (page 40).

Table 3.9: Signal Words and Phrases for Argument Elements

Element	Signal Words and Phrases
Claim	Describing words (such as *awful, amazing, beautiful, disgusting, miserable,* and *favorite*), modal verbs (such as *should, must,* and *ought to*), and superlatives (such as *best, worst, most,* and *smartest*)
Grounds	Cause and effect words (such as *because, as a result, due to, since,* and *for that reason*) and temporal transition words (such as *first, next,* and *finally*)
Backing	Illustrating transition words (such as *for example, for instance, to explain, to elaborate, specifically, in particular, such as, according to, as reported in,* and *as found by*)
Qualifiers	Concession words (such as *even if, despite the fact, albeit, admitting, granting, although, at any rate, at least, still, even though, granted that, while it may be true, in spite of, of course, just because . . . doesn't mean, necessarily,* and *whereas*)

Source: Rogers & Simms, 2015, p. 19.

Finally, teachers should present students with the various types of backing that might be used in an argument, such as those found in table 3.10.

Table 3.10: Different Types of Backing

Type of Backing	Definition	Examples
Expert Opinion	A statement made by an individual who is recognized as an expert in his or her field.	Someone with a doctorate in climatology and years of field-research experience offers an opinion on the severity of global warming. An experienced and successful director of Broadway plays offers an opinion on the quality of an acting performance. An official at the U.S. Federal Reserve offers an opinion on the state of the economy.
Research Results	Data collected through methodical investigation or through scientific experiments designed to test a hypothesis. Conclusions based on research results are not as unanimous and definitive as facts, but they come closer as more studies yield the same findings.	The U.S. Census Bureau reports working women's full-time earnings to be 75.7 percent of working men's earnings (DeNavas-Walt, Proctor, & Smith, 2012). The use of academic games in the classroom is associated with a gain of 20 percentile points in student achievement (Haystead & Marzano, 2009). About 20 percent of youth in grades 9–12 report being bullied at school (National Center for Injury Prevention and Control, 2012).
Factual Information	Information that has evidential support and is generally acknowledged to be proven or true.	The state flower of Montana is the bitterroot. The American Civil War began in 1861 and ended in 1865. Ladybugs help plants by eating pests such as aphids.

Source: Rogers & Simms, 2015, p. 19.

Tables 3.8, 3.9, and 3.10 present a relatively thorough breakdown of the different elements that compose an argument, along with clear examples. These elements are fundamental to students' understanding of argumentation. In effect, it is unwise and unfair to ask students to generate and support claims without directly teaching them how to do so. This is the case for any of the scientific and engineering practices that students are expected to utilize.

Many of the processes in the taxonomy presented in appendix A (page 127) pair nicely with the scientific and engineering practices. For example, the scientific and engineering practice of planning and carrying out investigations is virtually synonymous with the process of experimenting, found at level 4 (knowledge utilization) difficulty of the taxonomy. Additionally, the scientific and engineering practice of developing and using models is basically the same as the process of symbolizing, found at level 2 (comprehension) difficulty of the taxonomy. Strategies for teaching students to use all of the various taxonomy processes are well defined. For example, Robert J. Marzano and Debra J. Pickering (1997) and Robert J. Marzano and Tammy Heflebower (2012) offered the following process for experimenting.

1. Observe and describe something that occurs.

2. Try to explain the occurrence using information you already know or can find out.

3. Make a prediction based on your explanation.

4. Set up an experiment to test your prediction.

5. Adjust your explanation (if necessary) based on the results of the experiment.

This process for experimenting is just one of many that can be used to provide direct instruction for the various scientific and engineering practices.

Summary

This chapter reviewed how proficiency scales can be used to enhance classroom instruction. Teachers should consider three types of lessons when planning instruction—(1) direct instruction lessons, (2) practicing and deepening lessons, and (3) knowledge application lessons—along with instructional strategies that appear during all types of lessons. The lesson plan format in figure 3.1 (page 38) provided questions teachers can ask themselves when planning daily lessons. Finally, this chapter emphasized the need for direct instruction when teaching scientific and engineering practices and provided example resources a teacher might use during this direct instruction process. The following chapter examines how proficiency scales can be used to inform classroom assessment.

4

Proficiency Scales and Classroom Assessment

In addition to guiding classroom instruction, proficiency scales can also guide classroom assessment. Indeed, educators originally coined the term *measurement topic* because teachers found that proficiency scales served as useful assessment tools. This is primarily because the process of constructing a proficiency scale is very similar to the process test designers use when constructing an assessment.

Test Design

While there are many descriptions of the test design process (see Downing & Haladyna, 2006), all share at least two characteristics: (1) specification of content and (2) identification of the content's level of difficulty. These two features are depicted in table 4.1.

Table 4.1: Identification of Level of Difficulty of Content for Test Design

	Inheritance of Traits	**Variation of Traits**	**Adaptation**
Level 4 **Knowledge Utilization**			
Level 3 **Analysis**			
Level 2 **Comprehension**			
Level 1 **Retrieval**			

The content axis (horizontal axis) in table 4.1 identifies measurement topics for assessment. In table 4.1, these subjects include the measurement topics of Inheritance of Traits, Variation of Traits, and Adaptation. The difficulty axis (vertical axis) addresses how easy or hard the content will be. To identify the difficulty level of content, some type of taxonomy is typically used. Webb (2006) suggested the following levels of cognitive complexity: level 1 (recall), which includes the recall of simple information; level 2 (skill/concept), which requires students to make a decision in response to a problem or activity; level 3 (strategic thinking), which requires reasoning, planning, using evidence, or higher-level thinking; and level 4 (extended thinking), which requires higher-level, complex thinking over extended periods of time. However, table 4.1 implements the taxonomy described in tables 2.8 and 2.9 (pages 25–28) and appendix A (page 127).

If a test designer wanted to create an assessment that tests the content presented on the content axis of table 4.1 at various difficulty levels—such as those presented on the difficulty axis of table 4.1—the designer would need to articulate what content knowledge looks like at each level of difficulty on the difficulty axis. As such, the designer might write descriptors in the appropriate cells to facilitate the subsequent composition of test items.

Proficiency scales, as described in this book, can be likened to a single column in table 4.1. They represent content related to specific topics (which we refer to as measurement topics) for which three levels of difficulty have been identified for a particular grade level. To generate assessments from a proficiency scale, a teacher should identify the type of items, tasks, or other information-gathering techniques he or she will use to determine how students perform at each level of the scale. The results of all assessments, regardless of their type, should be used to provide feedback to students. We recommend using two types of assessments to provide feedback: (1) whole-class assessments and (2) individual student assessments.

Whole-Class Assessments

As their name implies, whole-class assessments determine how well a class, considered as a group, performs relative to a particular proficiency scale. With these types of assessments, scores are not recorded for individual students but are instead recorded for the class as a whole. The following two techniques can be used when assessing an entire class: (1) unrecorded assessments and (2) monitoring student responses.

Unrecorded Assessments

Unrecorded assessments are administered to students and scored, though the scores are not recorded for individual students. Rather, the data are aggregated to provide an idea of the overall standing of the class. Assessments of this nature commonly take the form of quizzes. To illustrate, consider the sample quiz in figure 4.1 on the score 2.0 content of the middle school proficiency scale for the measurement topic of Natural Selection.

The quiz in figure 4.1 tests students' proficiency with score 2.0 content only, as the quiz only addresses factual information about natural selection at the detail level. The teacher might administer this as an announced or unannounced quiz to a class as score 2.0 content on natural selection was being taught. The test would be administered and immediately scored by the students themselves. The teacher would then collect the tests and examine their results. However, he or she would not record each student's score in the gradebook. Rather, the teacher would set up some type of cut score, which would establish what constitutes adequate understanding of the score 2.0 content. For example, a teacher might establish a cut score of 80 percent, meaning that students who receive an 80 percent or higher on the assessment achieve the cut score. After the assessment, the teacher would record what proportion of the class met the cut score for that specific assessment. The class's overall progress with various difficulties of content could be represented using a chart such as the one shown in figure 4.2 (page 46). Visit **marzanoresearch.com /reproducibles** for a blank reproducible of figure 4.2.

1. Natural selection is:

    a. The process of certain species voluntarily moving out of a specific ecosystem

    b. The process in which certain organisms that are better adapted to their environment survive and produce more offspring than other organisms that are less suited to the same environment

    c. The process farmers use to select certain plants from which to breed the next generation of plants

    d. The process of specific organisms moving up or down the food chain

2. Which of the following phenomena could NOT be accurately attributed to natural selection?

    a. Insects becoming resistant to pesticides after a generation

    b. Giraffes with long necks outliving giraffes with short necks as specific grasses and shrubs die out until giraffes with longer necks are the dominant species

    c. The development of breeds such as the Chesapeake Bay Retriever, which are bred for specific traits that are useful to humans

    d. Male peacocks displaying their large and colorful tails, as these appendages serve as ornaments to attract mates

3. Which researcher developed the theory of evolution?

    a. Alfred Russel Wallace

    b. Reginald Punnett

    c. Albert Einstein

    d. Charles Darwin

4. Scientists believe that humans and apes are very similar in ancestry because:

    a. They share near-identical nucleotide sequences

    b. Both species have emotionally expressive eyes

    c. They share near-identical geographical points of origin

    d. Humans and apes share common characteristics, such as being highly social animals

5. Imagine a forest with a beetle that comes in two colors: red and brown. Birds that live in the forest begin to eat the red beetles because they are easily seen against tree bark. After many years without significant alterations to the ecosystem, which one of these outcomes is LEAST likely?

    a. The birds evolve to better see the brown beetles against the bark

    b. The brown beetles and red beetles thrive in similar numbers

    c. The brown beetles become the dominant species

    d. The red beetles slowly become more brown in color over time

Figure 4.1: Selected-response quiz on score 2.0 content of the middle school proficiency scale for the measurement topic of Natural Selection.

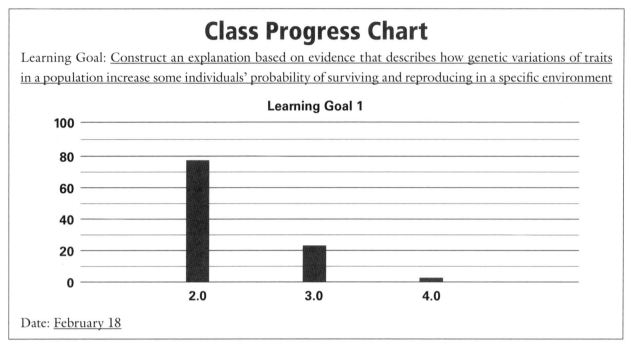

Class Progress Chart

Learning Goal: <u>Construct an explanation based on evidence that describes how genetic variations of traits in a population increase some individuals' probability of surviving and reproducing in a specific environment</u>

Learning Goal 1

Date: <u>February 18</u>

Source: Adapted from Marzano, 2010, p. 90.

Figure 4.2: Percentage of middle school class proficient with various levels of content for the measurement topic of Natural Selection.

Figure 4.2 shows how a teacher might record scores for a whole-class quiz on score 2.0, 3.0, and 4.0 content of a specific proficiency scale. It indicates that about 75 percent of students in the class achieved the cut score (80 percent) for the score 2.0 content on the quiz, about 22 percent reached the cut score for the score 3.0 content, and about 3 percent achieved the cut score for the score 4.0 content. Alternatively, a teacher could administer quizzes on only score 2.0 content until the vast majority of students meet the cut score, then move on to testing the score 3.0 content of the proficiency scale.

Monitoring Student Responses

Along with unrecorded assessments, a teacher might systematically monitor student responses to questions at specific score levels of a proficiency scale. In effect, this technique is tantamount to using oral questioning as a type of assessment. To illustrate, assume that a teacher generated a number of selected-response items for score 2.0 content, such as the questions in the quiz from figure 4.1 (page 45). Because each item has only four response options, the teacher might ask one of the questions orally and ask each student to hold up one or more fingers to signify which answer he or she thinks is correct (that is, hold up one finger for answer option a, two fingers for answer option b, and so on). The teacher would record the percentage of students who correctly answered the question. After asking multiple questions, the teacher would have an overall percentage of students who answered questions on score 2.0 content correctly. These data could be used in the same way as the scores on the unrecorded quiz—to represent the progress of the class toward proficiency with content at various levels of a scale.

The teacher may also use response cards, which elicit responses from all students simultaneously, as a variation to the previous approach. After passing out reusable materials to students (such as twelve-inch whiteboards), the teacher would ask a selected-response or short-response question. Students would then record their answers on their whiteboards and, upon the teacher's request, hold up their responses in a way that shows only the teacher. One of the advantages of response cards is that the short-answer responses can provide teachers with more data about students' understanding of a topic than selected-response answers.

Finally, technology-based response systems provide a variety of opportunities for teachers. These devices allow students to respond to questions simultaneously. Most electronic devices have keypads that allow students to cast their votes for answers to teacher-posed questions. A teacher could then project students' answers on a screen and discuss the responses or review the answers in private to get an idea of the class's progress with specific content. Although electronic responses are used mainly with selected-response items, these response systems can also test short-response items. Students simply use the keypads to type out their short responses and then submit them to the individual teacher for review.

Individual Student Assessments

When using proficiency scales to assess and provide feedback to individual students, teachers record the scores representing each student's current proficiency status in a gradebook. This allows for tracking of a student's growth over time in each topic for which a proficiency scale has been created. To illustrate, consider figure 4.3. Visit **marzanoresearch.com/reproducibles** for a blank reproducible of figure 4.3.

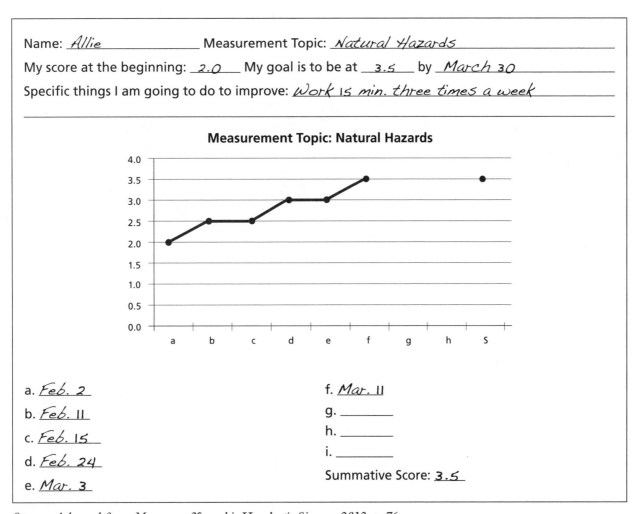

Source: Adapted from Marzano, Yanoski, Hoegh, & Simms, 2013, p. 76.

Figure 4.3: Individual student tracking chart for a proficiency scale for the measurement topic of Natural Hazards.

Figure 4.3 shows how a student might track his or her growth in a specific measurement topic over time. The student started with a score of 2.0 (shown in column a) and, at the end of the unit, ended with a score of 3.5 (shown in column f). Each score represents some type of assessment, with the summative score (shown in column s) representing the student's status at the end of the grading period. There are various types of assessments that are appropriate for generating individual student scores. Here, we address three types: (1) obtrusive assessments, (2) unobtrusive assessments, and (3) student-generated assessments.

Obtrusive Assessments

By definition, an obtrusive assessment generates scores for individual students by interrupting the flow of classroom instruction. In other words, instruction stops when assessment occurs. Obtrusive assessments often feature selected-response items (such as multiple-choice, matching, true/false, or fill-in-the-blank formats), constructed-response items (such as essays or short answers), or a combination of both. Obtrusive assessments can also take the form of oral responses (such as oral reports or probing discussions) or demonstrations (such as presentations or displays). While these different types of items can be used for any level of content in a proficiency scale, selected-response items are usually applied to score 2.0 content (see the quiz in figure 4.1, page 45). All other types of assessment items are more typically applied to score 3.0 and score 4.0 content in a proficiency scale. For example, the score 3.0 content of the kindergarten proficiency scale for the measurement topic of Natural Resources states that students will "use a model to represent the needs of different plants or animals (including humans) and the places they live." Teachers can address students' understanding of the content by asking them to write about their understanding (a short constructed-response item), to explain a model orally, or to provide a demonstration of their model.

Unobtrusive Assessments

Unobtrusive assessments, unlike obtrusive assessments, do not interrupt the flow of classroom instruction and can happen at any time. For this type of assessment, a teacher observes a student—without necessarily alerting the student to the fact that he or she is being assessed—and records an assessment score. Because unobtrusive assessments depend on silent observation, they are quite amenable to content involving skills, processes, or procedures. For example, assume a fifth-grade teacher has provided a specific laboratory protocol to help students "make observations and measurements to identify materials based on their properties" (a score 3.0 learning goal in the grade 5 proficiency scale for the measurement topic of Structure and Properties of Matter). As students apply the protocol to determine the properties of specific materials and to make educated guesses about the identities of the substances, the teacher walks around the room and observes students as they work. When the teacher observes a student providing clear evidence of a specific level of proficiency, the teacher records that score in a gradebook.

Teachers can also use unobtrusive assessments with informational content. For example, a middle school science teacher presents information about vestigial bones found in whales, and then asks the class to "apply scientific ideas to construct an explanation for the anatomical similarities and differences among modern organisms and between modern and fossil organisms to infer evolutionary relationships" (a score 3.0 learning goal in the middle school proficiency scale for the measurement topic of Evidence of Common Ancestry). The teacher divides the class into smaller groups and walks around the classroom as each of the groups discusses possible reasons for the presence of extra bones found in certain whales. The teacher listens as a student connects that these vestigial bones could have formerly been used as hind legs and proposes that perhaps whales originally lived on land. Convinced of the accuracy of the student's response, the teacher records a score of 3.0 for this student under the measurement topic of Evidence of Common Ancestry. The teacher could return to this group later and follow the discussion after the first student's initial hypothesis to grade other students based on their reactions to the suggestion.

Student-Generated Assessments

Student-generated assessments are assessments initiated and designed by students. These assessments confirm a student's movement up a proficiency scale from one score to another and are particularly powerful, as they put the student at the center of the assessment process. For example, during a unit on the measurement topic of Chemical Reactions, a high school science teacher might give students the opportunity to create student-generated assessments to show their proficiency with the score 3.0 content. A student who has already shown proficiency with score 2.0 content on the proficiency scale might design a student-generated assessment based off the performance expectation HS-PS1-2 (see Achieve, 2013a, p. 82), an element in the score 3.0 section that asks students to "construct and revise an explanation for the outcome of a simple chemical reaction based on the outermost electron states of atoms, trends in the periodic table, and knowledge of the patterns of chemical properties."

To demonstrate proficiency at this level, the student could use a valence-electron diagram to show that noble gases do not often interact with other atoms because they have full valence shells. The student might then compare the outer valence shell of a noble gas to the outer valence shells of other types of atoms before and after they are involved in chemical reactions to provide an explanation about the relationship between the stability of valence shells and chemical reactivity. The student could deliver his or her explanation in a one-on-one meeting, as a class presentation, or by video recording. If the teacher feels that the student has met the learning goal after reviewing the student's explanation, the teacher would assign that student a score of 3.0 under the measurement topic of Chemical Reactions. Again, the critical aspect of student-generated assessments is that students propose how they will demonstrate their own competence. Providing such opportunities not only enhances content knowledge, but also reinforces the nature and power of personal responsibility.

Creating Common Assessments Using Proficiency Scales

The proficiency scales in part II of this book (page 55) can also be used to design common assessments—assessments that attempt to ensure instructional consistency across classrooms and that collect formal data for professional learning community meetings. These data, once collected, inform the instructional practice within a school or district. An individual can use the following procedure—adapted from Marzano and colleagues (2013)—to develop high-quality common assessments.

1. **Identify the measurement topic to be assessed.** The score 2.0, 3.0, and 4.0 content from the proficiency scale selected provides the framework for designing the common assessment. The question to be answered in this step is: Where do we want students to be at the end of the learning process in relation to this measurement topic?

2. **Determine the number and type of assessment items for each level of the scale (an assessment blueprint).** It is important that an adequate number of assessment items are developed for each level on the scale to ensure that the data are trustworthy. Typically, at least three to five items per level are needed; an exception is the 4.0 level, which may only require one or two complex items. Also, when discussing potential item types, it is critical to consider the content being assessed in order to ensure a strong match between the assessment item and the content. While selected-response items can be useful for score 2.0

content, other forms (for example, constructed-response items) are typically more appropriate for score 3.0 and 4.0 content.

3. **Write the assessment items.** Make sure that the language used for the assessment items matches the language on the proficiency scale. This will ensure that the items truly measure students' proficiency with the skills and knowledge represented on the scale.

4. **Administer the common assessment, score it, and discuss the results.** Following test administration, the assessment is scored. Items can be coded as correct (C), partially correct (PC), or incorrect (I). Based on responses to the items, each student is assigned a score that correlates to a level on the proficiency scale. Assessment results can be used as the basis for discussion in a professional learning community meeting. The results can also be used to plan future instruction for individual students, small groups of students, or an entire class.

5. **Revise the assessment based on the data.** There are times when it becomes clear through data examination that an item is not of high quality. For example, if an item has no or very few correct responses or if a score 2.0 item is consistently answered incorrectly while a score 3.0 item related to the same skill or concept is consistently answered correctly by the same students, item revision may be necessary.

Recording Student Progress on Measurement Topics

Figure 4.4 depicts a chart that a teacher can use to track students' progress toward multiple learning goals over time. In figure 4.4, the teacher keeps track of students' scores for four different measurement topics (A, B, C, and D). The teacher enters the first assessment score for a specific measurement topic in the top left-hand corner of a cell and any additional scores related to the measurement topic immediately below it. If the teacher runs out of space, he or she creates a new column to the right of the first column. The box in the lower right-hand corner of each cell should contain the student's summative score for that specific measurement topic. A circle around a score indicates that a student was given an opportunity to raise his or her score from the circled assessment, whereas a square around a score shows that a teacher has judged this student to have reached a specific score level. Students with a square in one of their cells would not be expected to get a score lower than the score with a square around it within that specific measurement topic. Finally, *Inc.* indicates that a student did not complete a specific assessment.

To illustrate how these conventions are used, consider Janice's scores for measurement topic B. The first and second scores she received were both at the score 2.0 level. At this point, the teacher felt confident in Janice's proficiency with score 2.0 content, as shown by the square around the second assessment. However, for her third assessment, Janice received a score of 1.5, which would be considered uncharacteristic given Janice's previous performance. The teacher decided to give her an opportunity to raise the score of 1.5, as indicated by the circle around this score. Janice received a score of 2.5 on the fourth assessment, or the assessment opportunity to raise her uncharacteristic score on the third assessment. The teacher marked this in a new column immediately to the right of the first column because of space constraints.

Marshall and Walt have incomplete scores in measurement topic B and measurement topic D respectively. When a student misses or does not complete an assessment, the teacher notes that the assessment is incomplete, rather than recording a score of 0.0. This allows teachers to record only scores that provide a fair estimate of a student's overall proficiency with content in a particular measurement topic. As shown in the generic scale in table 2.1 (page 16), teachers can assign students a score of 0.0, which indicates that the students have no success with the content, even with help from a teacher. The use of *Inc.* in a teacher-tracking chart avoids confusion between these two different assessment results.

	Measurement Topic A		Measurement Topic B		Measurement Topic C		Measurement Topic D	
Janice	2.0		2.0	2.5	1.0		2.5	
	2.5		[2.0]		1.5		[2.5]	
	[2.5]		(1.5)		2.5		2.0	
Marshall	3.0	3.0	2.0		1.5		0.5	
	3.5		Inc.		[1.5]		1.5	
	(2.5)		3.0		2.0		2.5	
Lydia	2.5		2.0		2.5	3.0	2.5	3.0
	[2.5]		1.5		3.0		(1.0)	
	3.0		2.0		(2.0)		2.0	
Walt	2.0	3.0	2.5		3.0		3.0	
	(1.5)		[2.5]		3.5		[3.0]	
	2.5		3.0		4.0		Inc.	
Amar	1.5	2.0	1.5		(0.5)	1.5	3.5	
	2.0		2.0		1.0		[3.5]	
	(1.0)		2.5		1.5		3.5	

Source: Adapted from Marzano et al., 2013, p. 74.

Figure 4.4: Teacher-tracking chart for multiple students.

In order to determine a summative score, the teacher must examine the pattern of scores for each student in each measurement topic. Robert J. Marzano (2010) cautioned against teachers simply averaging a student's scores from an entire unit. Rather, a teacher should use the scores found within the cell to estimate a student's current score on the proficiency scale. For example, a teacher looking at Janice's performance during the unit on measurement topic D would see that Janice received a score of 2.0 on her last assessment. However, looking back over the course of the unit, the teacher would also see her previous proficiency with score 2.5 content. Using his or her judgment of Janice's familiarity with the content in measurement topic D, the teacher might assign Janice a summative score of 2.5.

It is important to note that there are many other ways to compute final summative scores for students (see Marzano, 2006, 2010). Technology-based programs exist that automatically compute summative scores for students using highly sophisticated mathematical and statistical techniques (see the Marzano Gradebook by Media-X at www.media-x.com/marzano-gradebook).

Grading and Reporting With Proficiency Scales

At the end of a grading period, teachers can use students' summative scores for each measurement topic to assign an overall grade in a specific subject area. While Marzano (2010) cautioned against averaging *within* a particular measurement topic to obtain a summative score, he noted it is perfectly acceptable to average scores *across* multiple measurement topics to obtain an overall grade for a particular subject. For example, consider a student who obtained the following summative scores in five measurement topics related to science: 2.5, 3.0, 3.5, 3.0, and 4.0. The average of those five scores—3.2—would serve as a good indication of the student's proficiency with the science content covered during the grading period.

In the previous scenario, the average score of 3.2 assumed that each summative score held the same weight. However, the teacher could decide to emphasize one measurement topic over the other measurement topics addressed during the grading period. To do so, the teacher would create a weighted average. With the scores given previously, the teacher might decide that the last measurement topic was doubly important in comparison to the others. The teacher would then include the last score of 4.0 twice when averaging, raising the student's average to 3.33. (For a more detailed discussion of standards-based grading, see Marzano, 2010.)

Since many schools and districts use traditional letter grades rather than four-point proficiency scales, teachers can use the conversion scale in table 4.2 to translate grades between the two systems.

Table 4.2: Conversion Scale Between Four-Point Proficiency Scales and Traditional Grades

Average Scale Score Across Multiple Measurement Topics	Traditional Grade
3.75–4.00	A+
3.26–3.74	A
3.00–3.25	A-
2.84–2.99	B+
2.67–2.83	B
2.50–2.66	B-
2.34–2.49	C+
2.17–2.33	C
2.00–2.16	C-
1.76–1.99	D+
1.26–1.75	D
1.00–1.25	D-
Below 1.00	F

Source: Marzano, 2010, p. 106.

The standards-based education movement has led many schools and districts to place emphasis on a student's growth over time. In a system aiming to emphasize student growth, a report card such as the one found in figure 4.5 may prove helpful.

The report card shown in figure 4.5 lists both letter grades and summative scores at the top and tracks a student's progress within each measurement topic for each subject at the bottom. The lower half of the report card indicates a student's summative score for individual measurement topics, whereas the shading scheme details a student's progress across a unit. For example, the student whose scores are reported in figure 4.5 began with a score of 1.0 for the measurement topic of Natural Resources, indicated by the boxes shaded in dark gray. However, by the end of the unit, the student had achieved a summative score of 3.0, which indicated a knowledge gain of 2.0 on the proficiency scale. The report card shows this progress through the light gray boxes that immediately follow the dark gray boxes, with the gray box furthest to the right indicating the student's final summative score for the unit.

Name: Allie Fairchild			Grade Level: 4		
Address: 123 Hawthorne Street Someplace, NY 12345			Teacher: Ms. Maple		
	Summative Score	Letter Grade		Summative Score	Letter Grade
Language Arts	2.88	B+	Science	3.20	A-
Mathematics	3.25	A-	Social Studies	2.25	C

English Language Arts										
	Summative Score	0.0	0.5	1.0	1.5	2.0	2.5	3.0	3.5	4.0
Questioning, Inference, and Interpretation	3.0									
Argumentation and Reasoning	2.5									
Research	3.5									
Grammar	2.5									

Mathematics										
	Summative Score	0.0	0.5	1.0	1.5	2.0	2.5	3.0	3.5	4.0
Fractions	4.0									
Adding and Subtracting Fractions	2.5									
Multiplication and Division	3.0									
Expression and Equations	3.5									

Science										
	Summative Score	0.0	0.5	1.0	1.5	2.0	2.5	3.0	3.5	4.0
Humans and Earth Systems	2.5									
Natural Resources	3.0									
Water and Earth's Surface	3.5									
Carbon Cycle	3.0									
Global Climate Change	4.0									

Social Studies										
	Summative Score	0.0	0.5	1.0	1.5	2.0	2.5	3.0	3.5	4.0
Cultural Relationships	2.5									
Physical Environments and Immigration	2.0									

Source: Adapted from Marzano et al., 2013, pp. 77–78.

Figure 4.5: Sample report card with traditional grades and progress tracking.

Conclusion

The measurement topics and proficiency scales presented in part II of this book have been derived from the Next Generation Science Standards (NGSS; Achieve, 2013a) in an attempt to create a tool that preserves both the intent and content of the NGSS and that classroom teachers at all grade levels can immediately put to use. The scales provide teachers with practical guidance for classroom instruction and assessment. Relative to instruction, the proficiency scales help teachers identify which content should be the focus of direct instruction, practicing and deepening, and knowledge application lessons. Relative to assessment, the proficiency scales lay the foundation for giving students meaningful feedback using either whole-class or individual student assessments.

Part II of this book provides the proficiency scales necessary for the type of instruction, assessment, and reporting described in this and previous chapters. In a similar work, *Using Common Core Standards to Enhance Classroom Instruction and Assessment* (Marzano et al., 2013), we present proficiency scales for English language arts and mathematics derived from the Common Core State Standards (NGA & CCSSO, 2010a, 2010b). These two sources, used in tandem, provide a foundation from which a school or district can redesign curriculum, instruction, and assessment around proficiency scales.

Part II

Scoring the New Science Standards

Proficiency Scales for the Next Generation Science Standards

As mentioned in part I, the proficiency scales created by Marzano Research were designed to include all of the performance expectations from the Next Generation Science Standards (NGSS; Achieve, 2013a). Here we include a brief explanation of performance expectation codes as well as a few notes about the scales.

Performance expectation codes cite the original performance expectation(s) upon which a scale is based. Each code identifies the grade level, discipline, core idea, and performance expectation number of the NGSS performance expectation associated with it.

The grade-level identifications are fairly straightforward. A number indicates a performance expectation's corresponding grade level (for example, 1 means grade 1), and K, MS, and HS indicate kindergarten, middle school, and high school, respectively.

The following letters indicate to which discipline from the NGSS a performance expectation belongs.

✦ Physical sciences = PS

✦ Life sciences = LS

✦ Earth and space sciences = ESS

✦ Engineering, technology, and applications of science = ETS

Although the NGSS named the fourth discipline *engineering, technology, and applications of science*, we simply refer to this discipline as *engineering*.

The number that immediately follows each discipline abbreviation indicates the disciplinary core idea to which a performance expectation belongs. A list of the core ideas that compose each discipline can be found in table 1.3 (page 9) or 1.4 (page 10) in the first chapter of part I of this book. The final number at the end of a performance expectation code signals which performance expectation within a core idea the code references.

Thus, the performance expectation code 4-PS3-2 (see Achieve, 2013a, p. 31) specifies that the performance expectation can be found at the fourth-grade level. The PS3 shows that the performance expectation comes from the discipline of physical sciences and the core idea of Energy. The 2 at the end of the performance expectation code identifies the performance expectation as the second performance expectation of the four found within the core idea of Energy at this grade level.

There is one performance expectation with an expanded performance expectation code. We divided the performance expectation HS-PS2-4 (see Achieve, 2013a, p. 84) into two parts—HS-PS2-4(a) and HS-PS2-4(b)—as the performance expectation references both Coulomb's law and Newton's law of gravitation. The original performance expectation defied classification within our organization system for proficiency scales, as we felt the two laws related to two different measurement topics. Thus, we divided the specific performance expectation into two parts and sorted them into the two appropriate measurement topics of (1) Electric and Magnetic Forces and (2) Gravity.

Any bolded text within a proficiency scale is taken directly from an NGSS performance expectation. We use bolded performance expectation codes in the score 2.0 section of each scale to indicate which elements at the score 2.0 level correspond with particular elements at the score 3.0 level.

Readers should also note that for each measurement topic, the proficiency scale for the highest grade level in a measurement topic displays all of the scores found in a typical proficiency scale (including half-point scores). For the proficiency scales at lower grade levels, the scale shows score 2.0 and 3.0 content only, as the descriptors for the other scores do not change from grade level to grade level.

Please note that the vocabulary terms found at the score 2.0 level of a proficiency scale are drawn directly from the NGSS performance expectations or the paraphrased example statements found at the score 3.0 level of a proficiency scale. However, key vocabulary terms from *Building Background Knowledge for Academic Achievement* (Marzano, 2004) have also been incorporated as score 2.0 content when appropriate.

Physical Sciences

Forces and Interactions

	High School
Score 4.0	In addition to score 3.0 performance, the student demonstrates in-depth inferences and applications that go beyond what was taught.
	Score 3.5 *In addition to score 3.0 performance, partial success at score 4.0 content*
Score 3.0	The student will: **HS-PS2-1—Analyze data to support the claim that Newton's second law of motion describes the mathematical relationship among the net force on a macroscopic object, its mass, and its acceleration** (for example, defend the claim that net force is equal to mass times acceleration by analyzing tables or graphs of position or velocity as a function of time for a falling object, an object rolling down a ramp, or a moving object being pulled by a constant force). **HS-PS2-2—Use mathematical representations to support the claim that the total momentum of a system of objects is conserved when there is no net force on the system** (for example, use mathematical formulas to defend the law of conservation of momentum—that the total momentum of a system of two macroscopic bodies moving in one dimension is conserved when it is not acted upon by outside forces). **HS-PS2-3—Apply scientific and engineering ideas to design, evaluate, and refine a device that minimizes the force on a macroscopic object during a collision** (for example, design a device—such as a football helmet or a parachute—meant to minimize force on a macroscopic object during a collision, make a qualitative assessment of the success of the device at protecting the object from damage, and modify the design to improve it).
	Score 2.5 *No major errors or omissions regarding score 2.0 content, and partial success at score 3.0 content*
Score 2.0	**HS-PS2-1**—The student will: • Recognize or recall specific vocabulary (for example, *acceleration, constant force, drag, force, Isaac Newton, law, macroscopic, mass, net force, Newtonian mechanics, Newton's second law of motion, position, relative motion, unbalanced force, velocity*). • Describe the key parts of Newton's second law of motion. • Describe the mathematical relationship between the net force on a macroscopic object, the object's mass, and the object's acceleration. **HS-PS2-2**—The student will: • Recognize or recall specific vocabulary (for example, *conservation, dimension, force, law of conservation of momentum, macroscopic, momentum, net force, system*). • Describe the key parts of the law of conservation of momentum. **HS-PS2-3**—The student will: • Recognize or recall specific vocabulary (for example, *collision, damage, design, device, evaluate, force, macroscopic, minimize, refine*). • Describe the forces acting on an object during a collision and the effect of those forces.
	Score 1.5 *Partial success at score 2.0 content, and major errors or omissions regarding score 3.0 content*
Score 1.0	With help, partial success at score 2.0 content and score 3.0 content
	Score 0.5 *With help, partial success at score 2.0 content but not at score 3.0 content*
Score 0.0	Even with help, no success

	Middle School
Score 3.0	The student will: **MS-PS2-1—Apply Newton's third law to design a solution to a problem involving the motion of two colliding objects** (for example, design a solution to a practical problem—such as two moving cars colliding, a car colliding with a stationary object, or a meteor and a space vehicle colliding—using the knowledge that every action has an equal and opposite reaction). **MS-PS2-2—Plan an investigation to provide evidence that the change in an object's motion depends on the sum of the forces on the object and the mass of the object** (for example, make qualitative comparisons of forces, masses, and changes in motion—changing only one variable at a time—to test Newton's first and third laws of motion).
Score 2.0	**MS-PS2-1**—The student will: • Recognize or recall specific vocabulary (for example, *collision, equal and opposite reaction, force, impact, Isaac Newton, motion, Newton's third law of motion, opposite force*). • Describe the key parts of Newton's third law of motion. **MS-PS2-2**—The student will: • Recognize or recall specific vocabulary (for example, *balanced force, change in motion, comparison, constant speed, control [variable], deceleration, dependent variable, direction of a force, direction of a motion, force, force strength, independent variable, inertia, mass, Newton's first law of motion, Newton's third law of motion, sum, variable*). • Describe how a change in an object's motion depends on the sum of the forces on the object and the mass of the object. • Make qualitative observations of the forces acting on an object.
	Grade 4
Score 3.0	The student will: **4-PS3-3—Ask questions and predict outcomes about the changes in energy that occur when objects collide** (for example, make qualitative predictions about the change in energy due to changes in speed as objects collide).
Score 2.0	**4-PS3-3**—The student will: • Recognize or recall specific vocabulary (for example, *change in energy, change in speed, collide, energy, friction, outcome, speed*). • Describe the relationship between speed and energy. • Describe what happens when objects collide.
	Grade 3
Score 3.0	The student will: **3-PS2-1—Plan and conduct an investigation to provide evidence of the effects of balanced and unbalanced forces on the motion of an object** (for example, test the relative, qualitative effects of balanced and unbalanced forces on the motion of an object, such as by pushing on one side of a ball to make it move versus pushing equally on opposite sides of a box to show that the box does not move at all). **3-PS2-2—Make observations and/or measurements of an object's motion to provide evidence that a pattern can be used to predict future motion** (for example, use observations of an object moving in a predictable pattern—such as a child swinging on a swing, a ball rolling back and forth in a bowl, or two children playing on a see-saw—to show that the future motion of the object can be predicted).

continued →

Score 2.0	**3-PS2-1**—The student will:
	• Recognize or recall specific vocabulary (for example, *applied force, balanced force, change of direction, change of motion, change of speed, effect, force, motion, unbalanced force*).
	• Describe balanced and unbalanced forces.
	• Describe the effect of force on the motion of an object.
	3-PS2-2—The student will:
	• Recognize or recall specific vocabulary (for example, *future motion, measure of motion, motion, past motion, pattern, position over time, predictable, relative position*).
	• Observe and describe the motion of various objects.
	• Describe patterns in the motion of various objects.

Kindergarten	
Score 3.0	The student will:
	K-PS2-1—**Plan and conduct an investigation to compare the effects of different strengths or different directions of pushes and pulls on the motion of an object** (for example, test and compare the relative, qualitative effects of pushing or pulling objects with varying strengths or in varying directions, such as a string pulling an object, a person pushing an object, a person stopping a rolling ball, or two objects colliding and pushing on each other).
	K-PS2-2—**Analyze data to determine if a design solution works as intended to change the speed or direction of an object with a push or a pull** (for example, make observations to determine whether using a ramp can help a ball travel a certain distance or whether using curved structures can cause a marble to turn and follow a particular path).
Score 2.0	**K-PS2-1**—The student will:
	• Recognize or recall specific vocabulary (for example, *collide, compare, different, direction, motion, pull, push, stop, strength*).
	• Demonstrate a push.
	• Demonstrate a pull.
	K-PS2-2—The student will:
	• Recognize or recall specific vocabulary (for example, *change, circular motion, curved, direction, distance, path, pull, push, ramp, speed, straight-line motion, turn, zigzag motion*).
	• Describe the speed and direction of an object.

Electric and Magnetic Forces

High School	
Score 4.0	In addition to score 3.0 performance, the student demonstrates in-depth inferences and applications that go beyond what was taught.
	Score 3.5 *In addition to score 3.0 performance, partial success at score 4.0 content*
Score 3.0	The student will:
	HS-PS2-4(b)—**Use mathematical representations of Coulomb's law to describe and predict the electrostatic forces between objects** (for example, use mathematical formulas to provide quantitative and conceptual explanations of Coulomb's law and to describe and predict the electrostatic force between two objects).
	HS-PS2-5—**Plan and conduct an investigation to provide evidence that an electric current can produce a magnetic field and that a changing magnetic field can produce an electric current** (for example, use teacher-provided materials and tools—such as copper coil, iron filings, and a magnet—to demonstrate the magnetic effect of an electric current and the principle of electromagnetic induction).

	Score 2.5	No major errors or omissions regarding score 2.0 content, and partial success at score 3.0 content
Score 2.0		**HS-PS2-4(b)**—The student will:

Score 2.0	**HS-PS2-4(b)**—The student will: • Recognize or recall specific vocabulary (for example, *Coulomb's law, electric current, electric field, electrostatic force, semiconductor, superconductor*). • Describe the key parts of Coulomb's law. • Describe the electrostatic forces between objects. **HS-PS2-5**—The student will: • Recognize or recall specific vocabulary (for example, *electric current, electric field, electrical energy, electromagnetic induction, magnet, magnetic effect, magnetic field, moving electrical charge, moving magnet*). • Describe the relationship between electric currents and magnetic fields.
	Score 1.5 — Partial success at score 2.0 content, and major errors or omissions regarding score 3.0 content
Score 1.0	With help, partial success at score 2.0 content and score 3.0 content
	Score 0.5 — With help, partial success at score 2.0 content but not at score 3.0 content
Score 0.0	Even with help, no success

Middle School

Score 3.0	The student will: **MS-PS2-3**—**Ask questions about data to determine the factors that affect the strength of electric and magnetic forces** (for example, investigate data—such as the effect of the number of turns of wire on the strength of an electromagnet or the effect of multiple magnets or magnets of varying strengths on the speed of an electric motor—and ask questions about them to figure out which factors affect the strength of electric and magnetic forces in devices like electromagnets, electric motors, or generators). **MS-PS2-5**—**Conduct an investigation and evaluate the experimental design to provide evidence that fields exist between objects exerting forces on each other even though the objects are not in contact** (for example, investigate firsthand experiences or simulations about objects that exert forces on each other, even when they are not in physical contact—such as the interaction of magnets, electrically charged strips of tape, or electrically charged pith balls—and use the results to give qualitative evidence for the existence of electric and magnetic fields).
Score 2.0	**MS-PS2-3**—The student will: • Recognize or recall specific vocabulary (for example, *effect, electric force, electric motor, electromagnet, factor, generator, magnetic force, speed, strength*). • Describe the effects of electric and magnetic forces. • Describe how certain devices use electric and magnetic forces. **MS-PS2-5**—The student will: • Recognize or recall specific vocabulary (for example, *contact, electric field, electrically charged, exert, field, force, interaction, magnet, magnetic field*). • Describe the effects of electric and magnetic fields on the forces of objects.

Grade 3

Score 3.0	The student will: **3-PS2-3**—**Ask questions to determine cause and effect relationships of electric or magnetic interactions between two objects not in contact with each other** (for example, figure out how the distance between objects affects the strength of an electric force when investigating the static electricity between two objects [such as the electrical force between hair and an electrically charged balloon or a charged rod and a piece of paper] and how the orientation of magnets affects the direction of the magnetic forces between two objects [such as the force between two permanent magnets, between an electromagnet and steel paperclips, or exerted by one magnet versus two magnets]). **3-PS2-4**—**Define a simple design problem that can be solved by applying scientific ideas about magnets** (for example, generate a design problem that can be solved with magnets, such as constructing a latch to keep a door shut or creating a device to keep two moving objects from touching each other).

continued →

Score 2.0	**3-PS2-3**—The student will:
	• Recognize or recall specific vocabulary (for example, *attraction, charge attraction, charge repulsion, charged rod, contact, direction, distance, electric interaction, electrical force, electrically charged, electromagnet, force, exert, magnet, magnetic attraction, magnetic force, magnetic interaction, magnetic repulsion, orientation, static electricity, strength*).
	• Describe the effects of electric and magnetic forces between two objects not in physical contact with each other.
	3-PS2-4—The student will:
	• Recognize or recall specific vocabulary (for example, *design problem, magnet, magnetic attraction, magnetic force, magnetic repulsion, orientation*).
	• Describe the qualitative effects of magnetic forces.

Gravity

High School		
Score 4.0	In addition to score 3.0 performance, the student demonstrates in-depth inferences and applications that go beyond what was taught.	
	Score 3.5	*In addition to score 3.0 performance, partial success at score 4.0 content*
Score 3.0	The student will: **HS-PS2-4(a)—Use mathematical representations of Newton's law of gravitation to describe and predict the gravitational forces between objects** (for example, use mathematical formulas to provide quantitative and conceptual explanations of Newton's law of gravitation and to predict the gravitational force between two objects).	
	Score 2.5	*No major errors or omissions regarding score 2.0 content, and partial success at score 3.0 content*
Score 2.0	**HS-PS2-4(a)**—The student will: • Recognize or recall specific vocabulary (for example, *conceptual explanation, gravitational energy, gravitational field, gravitational force, Isaac Newton, Newton's law of gravitation, quantitative explanation*). • Describe the key parts of Newton's law of gravitation. • Describe the gravitational forces between objects.	
	Score 1.5	*Partial success at score 2.0 content, and major errors or omissions regarding score 3.0 content*
Score 1.0	With help, partial success at score 2.0 content and score 3.0 content	
	Score 0.5	*With help, partial success at score 2.0 content but not at score 3.0 content*
Score 0.0	Even with help, no success	
Middle School		
Score 3.0	The student will: **MS-PS2-4—Construct and present arguments using evidence to support the claim that gravitational interactions are attractive and depend on the masses of interacting objects** (for example, use data generated from digital simulations or charts displaying mass, strength of interaction, distance from the sun, and orbital periods of objects within the solar system to defend the claim that gravitational interactions are attractive and dependent on the masses of interacting objects).	
Score 2.0	**MS-PS2-4**—The student will: • Recognize or recall specific vocabulary (for example, *attractive, direction of force, direction of motion, distance, gravitational force, gravitational interaction, interact, mass, orbital period, strength*). • Describe the effects of gravitational interactions. • Describe the role of mass in gravitational interactions.	

Grade 5	
Score 3.0	The student will: **5-PS2-1—Support an argument that the gravitational force exerted by Earth on objects is directed down** (for example, use evidence to show that an object near Earth's surface is drawn "down" to the center of the spherical planet due to its gravitational force).
Score 2.0	5-PS2-1—The student will: • Recognize or recall specific vocabulary (for example, *direction, Earth's gravity, Earth's rotation, Earth's surface, exert, gravitational force, gravity, sphere*). • Describe the relationship between Earth, gravity, and objects on Earth.

Energy and Forces

High School	
Score 4.0	In addition to score 3.0 performance, the student demonstrates in-depth inferences and applications that go beyond what was taught.
	Score 3.5 *In addition to score 3.0 performance, partial success at score 4.0 content*
Score 3.0	The student will: **HS-PS3-5—Develop and use a model of two objects interacting through electric or magnetic fields to illustrate the forces between objects and the changes in energy of the objects due to the interaction** (for example, create a diagram, text, or drawing of two objects interacting through electric or magnetic fields—such as a drawing of what happens when two charges of opposite polarity are near each other—to show how the forces between objects and the energy of objects change as a result of the interaction).
	Score 2.5 *No major errors or omissions regarding score 2.0 content, and partial success at score 3.0 content*
Score 2.0	HS-PS3-5—The student will: • Recognize or recall specific vocabulary (for example, *charge, electric field, energy, force, interact, magnetic field, polarity*). • Describe what happens when two objects interact through electric or magnetic fields.
	Score 1.5 *Partial success at score 2.0 content, and major errors or omissions regarding score 3.0 content*
Score 1.0	With help, partial success at score 2.0 content and score 3.0 content
	Score 0.5 *With help, partial success at score 2.0 content but not at score 3.0 content*
Score 0.0	Even with help, no success
Middle School	
Score 3.0	The student will: **MS-PS3-2—Develop a model to describe that when the arrangement of objects interacting at a distance changes, different amounts of potential energy are stored in the system** (for example, create a representation, picture, or written description to show that when an electric, magnetic, or gravitational interaction changes an arrangement of objects—such as a roller coaster cart at varying positions on a slope, the direction or orientation of a magnet, or a balloon charged with static electricity moving toward someone's hair—then the relative amounts of potential energy stored in that system also change).
Score 2.0	MS-PS3-2—The student will: • Recognize or recall specific vocabulary (for example, *arrangement, direction, distance, electric interaction, electrical charge, energy, interact, gravitational interaction, magnet, magnetic interaction, orientation, potential energy, static electricity, system*). • Describe how energy is stored in a system.

Energy Definitions

High School	
Score 4.0	In addition to score 3.0 performance, the student demonstrates in-depth inferences and applications that go beyond what was taught.
	Score 3.5 *In addition to score 3.0 performance, partial success at score 4.0 content*
Score 3.0	The student will: **HS-PS3-1—Create a computational model to calculate the change in the energy of one component in a system when the change in energy of the other component(s) and energy flows in and out of the system are known** (for example, use basic algebraic expressions or computations to calculate the change in the energy—thermal, kinetic, or within a gravitational, magnetic, or electric field—of one component in a two- or three-component system, given energy flows in and out of the system and changes in energy of the other component(s), and explain the meaning of mathematical expressions used in the model). **HS-PS3-2—Develop and use models to illustrate that energy at the macroscopic scale can be accounted for as a combination of energy associated with the motions of particles (objects) and energy associated with the relative position of particles (objects)** (for example, create a diagram, drawing, or computer simulation that shows that energy at the macroscopic scale—such as the conversion of kinetic energy to thermal energy or the energy stored due to the position of an object above the Earth or between two electrically charged plates—can be accounted for as either the motion of particles or energy stored in fields). **HS-PS3-3—Design, build, and refine a device that works within given constraints to convert one form of energy into another form of energy** (for example, based on qualitative and quantitative evaluations, use teacher-provided materials to design, build, and refine a device that works within given constraints [such as use of renewable energy forms, efficiency requirements, and so on] to convert one form of energy into another form [such as a Rube Goldberg device, wind turbine, solar cell, solar oven, or generator]).
	Score 2.5 *No major errors or omissions regarding score 2.0 content, and partial success at score 3.0 content*
Score 2.0	**HS-PS3-1**—The student will: • Recognize or recall specific vocabulary (for example, *algebraic expression, component, electric field, energy, flow, gravitational field, kinetic energy, magnetic field, renewable energy, system, thermal energy*). • State the basic algebraic expression or computation for calculating a change in energy. • Describe how the energy of one component in a two- or three-component system relates to the energy of the other components. **HS-PS3-2**—The student will: • Recognize or recall specific vocabulary (for example, *conversion, electrically charged, energy, field, kinetic energy, macroscopic scale, molecular energy, motion, particle, position, relative, thermal energy*). • Describe how energy results from the motion of particles (objects). • Describe how energy is stored in fields. **HS-PS3-3**—The student will: • Recognize or recall specific vocabulary (for example, *constraint, convert, device, efficient, energy, form, generator, renewable energy, Rube Goldberg device, solar cell, solar oven, wind turbine*). • Research ways in which energy can be converted from one form to another.
	Score 1.5 *Partial success at score 2.0 content, and major errors or omissions regarding score 3.0 content*
Score 1.0	With help, partial success at score 2.0 content and score 3.0 content
	Score 0.5 *With help, partial success at score 2.0 content but not at score 3.0 content*
Score 0.0	Even with help, no success

Middle School	
Score 3.0	The student will: **MS-PS3-1—Construct and interpret graphical displays of data to describe the relationships of kinetic energy to the mass of an object and to the speed of an object** (for example, create graphs that describe the difference between the relationship of kinetic energy and mass and the relationship of kinetic energy and speed, such as riding a bicycle at different speeds, rolling differently sized rocks downhill, or being hit by a Wiffle ball versus a tennis ball).
Score 2.0	**MS-PS3-1**—The student will: • Recognize or recall specific vocabulary (for example, *kinetic energy*, *mass*, *relationship*, *speed*). • Describe the relationship between the kinetic energy of an object and the mass of an object. • Describe the relationship between the kinetic energy of an object and the speed of an object.
Grade 4	
Score 3.0	The student will: **4-PS3-1—Use evidence to construct an explanation relating the speed of an object to the energy of that object** (for example, use qualitative measures of changes in speed to explain how speed relates to energy).
Score 2.0	**4-PS3-1**—The student will: • Recognize or recall specific vocabulary (for example, *change*, *energy*, *relate*, *speed*). • Describe the qualitative relationship between the energy of an object and the speed of an object.

Energy Conservation and Energy Transfer

High School		
Score 4.0	In addition to score 3.0 performance, the student demonstrates in-depth inferences and applications that go beyond what was taught.	
	Score 3.5	*In addition to score 3.0 performance, partial success at score 4.0 content*
Score 3.0	The student will: **HS-PS3-4—Plan and conduct an investigation to provide evidence that the transfer of thermal energy when two components of different temperature are combined within a closed system results in a more uniform energy distribution among the components in the system (second law of thermodynamics)** (for example, use teacher-provided materials and tools to conduct an investigation in which two components of different temperatures are combined within a closed system—such as mixing liquids at different initial temperatures or adding objects at different temperatures to water—and analyze data from the investigation using mathematical thinking to describe the energy changes both quantitatively and conceptually).	
	Score 2.5	*No major errors or omissions regarding score 2.0 content, and partial success at score 3.0 content*
Score 2.0	**HS-PS3-4**—The student will: • Recognize or recall specific vocabulary (for example, *closed system*, *component*, *conceptual*, *energy change*, *energy distribution*, *quantitative*, *second law of thermodynamics*, *system*, *temperature*, *thermal energy*, *thermal equilibrium*, *transfer*, *uniform*). • Describe the key parts of the second law of thermodynamics.	
	Score 1.5	*Partial success at score 2.0 content, and major errors or omissions regarding score 3.0 content*
Score 1.0	With help, partial success at score 2.0 content and score 3.0 content	
	Score 0.5	*With help, partial success at score 2.0 content but not at score 3.0 content*
Score 0.0	Even with help, no success	

continued →

Middle School	
Score 3.0	The student will: **MS-PS3-3—Apply scientific principles to design, construct, and test a device that either minimizes or maximizes thermal energy transfer** (for example, design and build a device that minimizes or maximizes thermal energy transfer—such as an insulated box, a solar cooker, or a polystyrene cup—and then assess the success of the device). **MS-PS3-4—Plan an investigation to determine the relationships among the energy transferred, the type of matter, the mass, and the change in the average kinetic energy of the particles as measured by the temperature of the sample** (for example, design and conduct an experiment that compares the temperature change of samples of different materials with the same mass as they cool or heat in an environment or of objects of the same material with different masses when a specific amount of energy is added—such as by comparing final water temperatures after different masses of ice have melted in the same volume of water with the same initial temperature—to investigate the relationships between energy transfer, type of matter, mass, and change in average kinetic energy). **MS-PS3-5—Construct, use, and present arguments to support the claim that when the kinetic energy of an object changes, energy is transferred to or from the object** (for example, use empirical evidence—such as an inventory or other representation of energy before and after a transfer in the form of a change in temperature or motion of an object—to support the claim that when kinetic energy changes, energy is transferred).
Score 2.0	**MS-PS3-3—**The student will: • Recognize or recall specific vocabulary (for example, *device, energy transfer, insulated, maximize, minimize, temperature, thermal energy*). • Describe thermal energy transfer. **MS-PS3-4—**The student will: • Recognize or recall specific vocabulary (for example, *average, change, cool, energy, environment, heat, heat convection, heat energy, heat radiation, heat retention, initial, kinetic energy, mass, material, matter, particle, relationship, sample, temperature, transfer, volume*). • State accurate information about energy transfer, types of matter, mass, and changes in the average kinetic energy of particles. **MS-PS3-5—**The student will: • Recognize or recall specific vocabulary (for example, *change, conservation of energy, energy, inventory, kinetic energy, motion, motion energy, representation, temperature, transfer*). • Describe how motion energy is transferred to and from an object.
Grade 4	
Score 3.0	The student will: **4-PS3-2—Make observations to provide evidence that energy can be transferred from place to place by sound, light, heat, and electric currents** (for example, use qualitative observations as evidence that energy can be transferred from place to place by sound, light, heat, and electric currents). **4-PS3-4—Apply scientific ideas to design, test, and refine a device that converts energy from one form to another** (for example, design, test, and refine a device—such as an electric circuit that converts electrical energy into motion, light, or sound or a passive solar heater that converts light into heat—that works within given constraints of material, cost, or time to convert motion energy to electrical energy or to use stored energy to cause motion or produce light or sound).

Score 2.0	4-PS3-2—The student will:
	• Recognize or recall specific vocabulary (for example, *conduction, conductivity, electric current, energy, heat, light, sound, transfer*).
	• Identify examples of energy being transferred from one place to another.
	4-PS3-4—The student will:
	• Recognize or recall specific vocabulary (for example, *constraint, convert, device, electric circuit, electrical energy, form, heat, light, light absorption, motion, motion energy, sound, stored energy*).
	• Describe the different forms of energy.
	• Identify examples of energy being converted from one form into another (such as electrical energy being converted into motion energy or of light energy being converted into heat).

Kindergarten	
Score 3.0	The student will:
	K-PS3-1—Make observations to determine the effect of sunlight on Earth's surface (for example, make relative observations—such as "warmer" and "cooler"—of the effect of sunlight on sand, soil, rocks, and water to make generalizations about the effect that sunlight has on Earth's surface).
	K-PS3-2—Use tools and materials to design and build a structure that will reduce the warming effect of sunlight on an area (for example, use teacher-provided tools and materials to design and build a structure—such as an umbrella, canopy, or tent—that reduces the warming effect of the sun).
Score 2.0	**K-PS3-1**—The student will:
	• Recognize or recall specific vocabulary (for example, *cold, cooler, Earth's surface, effect, hot, observation, rock, sand, soil, sunlight, warmer, water*).
	• Describe the relative temperatures of objects using words like *cold, warmer, hot*, and *cooler*.
	• Describe the effect of the sun on an object.
	K-PS3-2—The student will:
	• Recognize or recall specific vocabulary (for example, *area, reduce, structure, sun, sunlight, warming effect*).
	• Identify objects that provide shade from the sun (such as a tree or porch).

Waves

High School		
Score 4.0	In addition to score 3.0 performance, the student demonstrates in-depth inferences and applications that go beyond what was taught.	
	Score 3.5	*In addition to score 3.0 performance, partial success at score 4.0 content*
Score 3.0	The student will:	
	HS-PS4-1—Use mathematical representations to support a claim regarding relationships among the frequency, wavelength, and speed of waves traveling in various media (for example, use qualitative descriptions of algebraic relationships to explain the relationships between the frequency, wavelength, and speed of waves traveling in various media, such as electromagnetic radiation traveling in a vacuum versus through glass, sound waves traveling through air versus water, or seismic waves traveling through the Earth).	
	Score 2.5	*No major errors or omissions regarding score 2.0 content, and partial success at score 3.0 content*

continued →

Score 2.0	HS-PS4-1—The student will: • Recognize or recall specific vocabulary (for example, *algebraic, electromagnetic radiation, frequency, medium, properties of waves, relationship, seismic wave, sound wave, speed, travel, vacuum, wave, wave packet, wave source, wavelength*). • Describe the relationship between the frequency, wavelength, and speed of waves.
	Score 1.5	*Partial success at score 2.0 content, and major errors or omissions regarding score 3.0 content*
Score 1.0	With help, partial success at score 2.0 content and score 3.0 content
	Score 0.5	*With help, partial success at score 2.0 content but not at score 3.0 content*
Score 0.0	Even with help, no success

Middle School	
Score 3.0	The student will: **MS-PS4-1—Use mathematical representations to describe a simple model for waves that includes how the amplitude of a wave is related to the energy in a wave** (for example, use mathematical formulas and qualitative thinking to describe standard repeating waves, including how the amplitude of a wave relates to the energy in a wave). **MS-PS4-2—Develop and use a model to describe that waves are reflected, absorbed, or transmitted through various materials** (for example, create a drawing, simulation, or written description that explains—qualitatively—how light waves and mechanical waves are reflected, absorbed, or transmitted through various materials).
Score 2.0	MS-PS4-1—The student will: • Recognize or recall specific vocabulary (for example, *amplitude, energy, relate, standard, wave*). • Describe the relationship between the amplitude and energy of a wave. MS-PS4-2—The student will: • Recognize or recall specific vocabulary (for example, *absorb, frequency, light wave, matter wave, mechanical wave, reflect, sound wave, transmit, water wave, wave*). • Describe the reflection, absorption, and transmission of waves.

Grade 4	
Score 3.0	The student will: **4-PS4-1—Develop a model of waves to describe patterns in terms of amplitude and wavelength and that waves can cause objects to move** (for example, create a diagram, analogy, or physical model using wire that describes qualitative patterns of amplitude and wavelength and that shows that waves can cause objects to move).
Score 2.0	4-PS4-1—The student will: • Recognize or recall specific vocabulary (for example, *amplitude, pattern, properties of sound, wave, wavelength*). • Describe the parts of waves (for example, amplitude and wavelength). • Describe the motion of an object being moved by a wave.

Grade 1	
Score 3.0	The student will: **1-PS4-1—Plan and conduct investigations to provide evidence that vibrating materials can make sound and that sound can make materials vibrate** (for example, conduct an experiment to show that vibrating materials—such as tuning forks and plucked, stretched strings—can make sound and that sound can make materials vibrate—such as a piece of paper held near a speaker or an object held near a vibrating tuning fork).
Score 2.0	1-PS4-1—The student will: • Recognize or recall specific vocabulary (for example, *sound, tuning fork, vibration*). • Identify examples of materials that vibrate to produce sound. • Describe what it means for something to vibrate.

Electromagnetic Radiation

	High School	
Score 4.0	In addition to score 3.0 performance, the student demonstrates in-depth inferences and applications that go beyond what was taught.	
	Score 3.5	*In addition to score 3.0 performance, partial success at score 4.0 content*
Score 3.0	The student will: **HS-PS4-3—Evaluate the claims, evidence, and reasoning behind the idea that electromagnetic radiation can be described either by a wave model or a particle model, and that for some situations one model is more useful than the other** (for example, determine whether experimental evidence supports the claim that electromagnetic radiation can be described by either a wave model or a particle model, as well as the claim that for different phenomena—such as resonance, interference, diffraction, and photoelectric effect—one model is more useful than the other). **HS-PS4-4—Evaluate the validity and reliability of claims in published materials of the effects that different frequencies of electromagnetic radiation have when absorbed by matter** (for example, evaluate the validity and reliability of claims in trade books, magazines, web resources, videos, and other passages that may reflect bias about the idea that photons associated with different frequencies of light have different energies or that the damage to living tissue from electromagnetic radiation depends on the energy of the radiation).	
	Score 2.5	*No major errors or omissions regarding score 2.0 content, and partial success at score 3.0 content*
Score 2.0	**HS-PS4-3—**The student will: <ul><li>Recognize or recall specific vocabulary (for example, *diffraction, electromagnetic, electromagnetic field, electromagnetic radiation, electromagnetic wave, experimental evidence, interference, model, particle model, phenomenon, photoelectric effect, resonance, wave model*).</li><li>Describe the wave model of electromagnetic radiation.</li><li>Describe the particle model of electromagnetic radiation.</li><li>Summarize the claims and reasoning behind the idea that electromagnetic radiation can be described either by a wave model or a particle model.</li></ul> **HS-PS4-4—**The student will: <ul><li>Recognize or recall specific vocabulary (for example, *absorb, bias, damage, effect, electromagnetic radiation, energy, frequency, infrared radiation, light, living tissue, matter, photon, radiation*).</li><li>Summarize claims about the effects that different frequencies of electromagnetic radiation have when absorbed by matter.</li></ul>	
	Score 1.5	*Partial success at score 2.0 content, and major errors or omissions regarding score 3.0 content*
Score 1.0	With help, partial success at score 2.0 content and score 3.0 content	
	Score 0.5	*With help, partial success at score 2.0 content but not at score 3.0 content*
Score 0.0	Even with help, no success	
	Grade 4	
Score 3.0	**4-PS4-2—Develop a model to describe that light reflecting from objects and entering the eye allows objects to be seen** (for example, create a model that shows how light reflecting off of an object enters the eye and allows an object to be seen).	
Score 2.0	**4-PS4-2—**The student will: <ul><li>Recognize or recall specific vocabulary (for example, *eye, light, reflect*).</li><li>Describe the reflection of light off of an object.</li></ul>	

continued →

Grade 1	
Score 3.0	**1-PS4-2—Make observations to construct an evidence-based account that objects can be seen only when illuminated** (for example, make observations in a completely dark room, with a pinhole box, or about a video of a cave explorer with a flashlight, and use those observations to support the claim that objects can only be seen when they are illuminated, either from an external light source or by an object giving off its own light). **1-PS4-3—Plan and conduct an investigation to determine the effect of placing objects made with different materials in the path of a beam of light** (for example, conduct an experiment to figure out what happens when objects that have different transparencies—whether they are fully transparent, such as clear plastic; translucent, such as wax paper; opaque, such as cardboard; or reflective, such as a mirror—are placed in the path of a beam of light).
Score 2.0	**1-PS4-2**—The student will: • Recognize or recall specific vocabulary (for example, *evidence-based, external, illuminate, internal, light, light source*). • State examples of objects that produce light. **1-PS4-3**—The student will: • Recognize or recall specific vocabulary (for example, *effect, light, light beam, light source, opaque, path, properties of light, reflective, shadow, translucent, transparent*). • Describe the effect of a beam of light shining on an object.

Information Technologies

High School	
Score 4.0	In addition to score 3.0 performance, the student demonstrates in-depth inferences and applications that go beyond what was taught.
	Score 3.5	*In addition to score 3.0 performance, partial success at score 4.0 content*
Score 3.0	The student will: **HS-PS4-2—Evaluate questions about the advantages of using a digital transmission and storage of information** (for example, evaluate questions about the advantages of digitally transmitting and storing information [such as the stability of digital information due to its ability to be transferred easily, copied and shared rapidly, and stored reliably in computer memory] as well as the disadvantages [such as issues of easy deletion, security, and theft]). **HS-PS4-5—Communicate technical information about how some technological devices use the principles of wave behavior and wave interactions with matter to transmit and capture information and energy** (for example, use qualitative information to explain how some technological devices use waves to transmit and capture information and energy, such as solar cells and technology for medical imaging and communications).
	Score 2.5	*No major errors or omissions regarding score 2.0 content, and partial success at score 3.0 content*
Score 2.0	**HS-PS4-2**—The student will: • Recognize or recall specific vocabulary (for example, *advantage, digital transmission, digitize, disadvantage, information, memory, pixel, security, stable, store, transfer, transmission*). • Describe the advantages and disadvantages of digital transmission and storage of information. **HS-PS4-5**—The student will: • Recognize or recall specific vocabulary (for example, *capture, communications technology, convert, electricity, energy, information, matter, medical imaging, principle, solar cell, technical information, technological device, transmit, wave, wave behavior, wave interaction*). • Describe the use of waves to transmit and capture information and energy.
	Score 1.5	*Partial success at score 2.0 content, and major errors or omissions regarding score 3.0 content*

Score 1.0	With help, partial success at score 2.0 content and score 3.0 content	
	Score 0.5	*With help, partial success at score 2.0 content but not at score 3.0 content*
Score 0.0	Even with help, no success	

Middle School	
Score 3.0	The student will: **MS-PS4-3—Integrate qualitative scientific and technical information to support the claim that digitized signals are a more reliable way to encode and transmit information than analog signals** (for example, make and defend the claim that using digitized signals—such as fiber-optic cables transmitting light pulses, Wi-Fi devices using radio wave pulses, or the conversion of stored binary patterns making sound or text on a computer screen—are more reliable than analog signals when it comes to communicating information).
Score 2.0	**MS-PS4-3**—The student will: • Recognize or recall specific vocabulary (for example, *analog signal, binary pattern, conversion, digitized signal, encode, fiber-optic cable, information, light pulse, radio wave, reliable, transmit, wave pulse, Wi-Fi device*). • Describe how digitized signals encode and transmit information. • Describe the advantages and disadvantages of communicating using digitized and analog signals.

Grade 4	
Score 3.0	The student will: **4-PS4-3—Generate and compare multiple solutions that use patterns to transfer information** (for example, figure out different ways to transfer information using patterns—such as sending coded information through the sound waves produced by a drum, using a grid of 1's and 0's representing black and white to send information about a picture, or using Morse code to send text—and compare these different methods).
Score 2.0	**4-PS4-3**—The student will: • Recognize or recall specific vocabulary (for example, *coded, compare, convert, decode, information, Morse code, pattern, sound wave, transfer*). • Describe patterns that humans use to transfer information.

Grade 1	
Score 3.0	The student will: **1-PS4-4—Use tools and materials to design and build a device that uses light or sound to solve the problem of communicating over a distance** (for example, design a device that allows people to communicate over a distance—such as signals through light flashes, a paper cup and string "telephone," or a pattern of drum beats—and construct the device using tools and materials).
Score 2.0	**1-PS4-4**—The student will: • Recognize or recall specific vocabulary (for example, *communicate, construct, device, distance, light, light source, pattern, signal, sound*). • Identify different devices that use light or sound to communicate.

States of Matter

Middle School	
Score 4.0	In addition to score 3.0 performance, the student demonstrates in-depth inferences and applications that go beyond what was taught.
	Score 3.5	*In addition to score 3.0 performance, partial success at score 4.0 content*

continued →

Score 3.0	The student will:
	MS-PS1-4—Develop a model that predicts and describes changes in particle motion, temperature, and state of a pure substance when thermal energy is added or removed (for example, create a qualitative, molecular-level drawing or diagram of a solid, liquid, or gas [such as water, carbon dioxide, or helium] to show that adding or removing thermal energy increases or decreases the kinetic energy of particles [such as molecules or inert atoms] until a change of state occurs).

	Score 2.5	*No major errors or omissions regarding score 2.0 content, and partial success at score 3.0 content*

Score 2.0	**MS-PS1-4**—The student will:
	• Recognize or recall specific vocabulary (for example, *atom, atomic motion, change, change of state, decrease, gas, increase, inert atom, kinetic energy, liquid, molecular level, molecular motion, molecule, particle, particle motion, pure substance, solid, state, temperature, thermal energy*).
	• Describe the changes that occur in particle motion, temperature, and state when thermal energy is added or removed.

	Score 1.5	*Partial success at score 2.0 content, and major errors or omissions regarding score 3.0 content*

Score 1.0	With help, partial success at score 2.0 content and score 3.0 content

	Score 0.5	*With help, partial success at score 2.0 content but not at score 3.0 content*

Score 0.0	Even with help, no success

Grade 2	
Score 3.0	The student will:
	2-PS1-4—Construct an argument with evidence that some changes caused by heating or cooling can be reversed and some cannot (for example, make and defend the claim that some changes caused by heating or cooling can be reversed and some cannot—such as by melting and freezing water or butter to show reversible changes and cooking an egg, freezing a plant leaf, or burning paper to show irreversible changes).
Score 2.0	**2-PS1-4**—The student will:
	• Recognize or recall specific vocabulary (for example, *change, cool, freeze, heat, irreversible, melt, reversible, temperature*).
	• Describe different types of changes that can be caused by heating.
	• Describe different types of changes that can be caused by cooling.

Structure and Properties of Matter

High School	
Score 4.0	In addition to score 3.0 performance, the student demonstrates in-depth inferences and applications that go beyond what was taught.

	Score 3.5	*In addition to score 3.0 performance, partial success at score 4.0 content*

Score 3.0	The student will:
	HS-PS1-1—Use the periodic table as a model to predict the relative properties of elements based on the patterns of electrons in the outermost energy level of atoms (for example, use information on the periodic table to predict relative properties—such as the reactivity of metals, types of bonds formed, number of bonds formed, and reaction with oxygen—of main group elements).
	HS-PS1-3—Plan and conduct an investigation to gather evidence to compare the structure of substances at the bulk scale to infer the strength of electrical forces between particles (for example, figure out the strength of electrical forces between ions, atoms, molecules, or networked materials—such as graphite—by investigating the structure and characteristics of different substances at the bulk scale, including melting point, boiling point, vapor pressure, and surface tension).

	HS-PS2-6—Communicate scientific and technical information about why the molecular-level structure is important in the functioning of designed materials (for example, use teacher-provided molecular-level structures of specific designed materials—such as electrically conductive metals, flexible but durable materials, and pharmaceuticals designed to interact with specific receptors—to explain how attractive and repulsive forces at the molecular level determine function).
Score 2.5	*No major errors or omissions regarding score 2.0 content, and partial success at score 3.0 content*

Score 2.0

HS-PS1-1—The student will:

- Recognize and recall specific vocabulary (for example, *atom, atomic mass, atomic nucleus, atomic number, bond, electron, element, element stability, elements of matter, main group element, model, neutron, outermost energy level, pattern, periodic table, predict, property, proton, reaction, reactivity, relative, relative mass, weight of subatomic particles*).
- Use the periodic table to gather information about main group elements.

HS-PS1-3—The student will:

- Recognize and recall specific vocabulary (for example, *atom, atomic energy, boiling point, bulk scale, characteristic, electrical force, elementary particle, ion, melting point, molecule, networked material, particle, strength, structure, substance, surface tension, vapor pressure*).
- Model the structures of various substances.
- Describe the relationship between electrical forces and particles.

HS-PS2-6—The student will:

- Recognize or recall specific vocabulary (for example, *attractive, designed material, durable, electrically conductive, electron configuration, electron sharing, electron transfer, flexible, force, formation of polymers, function, ionic motion, isotope, molecular arrangement, molecular level, molecular motion, pharmaceutical, receptor, repulsive, structure, synthetic polymer*).
- Describe the structure of different substances at the molecular level.
- Describe the relationship between attractive and repulsive forces at the molecular level.

Score 1.5	*Partial success at score 2.0 content, and major errors or omissions regarding score 3.0 content*
Score 1.0	With help, partial success at score 2.0 content and score 3.0 content
Score 0.5	*With help, partial success at score 2.0 content but not at score 3.0 content*
Score 0.0	Even with help, no success

Middle School

Score 3.0

The student will:

MS-PS1-1—Develop models to describe the atomic composition of simple molecules and extended structures (for example, create molecular-level drawings, three-dimensional ball-and-stick structures, or computer representations to describe the atomic composition of simple molecules [such as ammonia and methanol] and extended structures [such as sodium chloride or diamonds]).

Score 2.0

MS-PS1-1—The student will:

- Recognize or recall specific vocabulary (for example, *actual mass, atom, atomic composition, atomic weight, extended structure, molecular arrangement, molecular level, molecule, simple molecule, three-dimensional*).
- Describe the individual components of the atomic composition of molecules.

Grade 5

Score 3.0

The student will:

5-PS1-1—Develop a model to describe that matter is made of particles too small to be seen (for example, show that matter is made of microscopic particles by adding air to expand a basketball, compressing air in a syringe, dissolving sugar in water, or evaporating salt water).

5-PS1-3—Make observations and measurements to identify materials based on their properties (for example, identify various materials—such as baking soda and other powders, metals, minerals, and liquids—based on their color, hardness, reflectivity, electrical conductivity, thermal conductivity, solubility, and response to magnetic forces).

continued →

Score 2.0	**5-PS1-1**—The student will:
	• Recognize or recall specific vocabulary (for example, *compress, dissolve, evaporate, expand, matter, microscopic, particle*).
	• Describe how matter is constructed of many parts.
	5-PS1-3—The student will:
	• Recognize or recall specific vocabulary (for example, *classification of substances, color, electrical conductivity, hardness, magnetic force, material, property, reflectivity, response, solubility, thermal conductivity*).
	• Describe the properties scientists use to identify materials.
	• Observe and describe the properties of different materials (for example, color, hardness, reflectivity, electrical conductivity, thermal conductivity, response to magnetic forces, and solubility).

Grade 2	
Score 3.0	The student will:
	2-PS1-1—**Plan and conduct an investigation to describe and classify different kinds of materials by their observable properties** (for example, observe and describe the color, texture, hardness, and flexibility of different kinds of materials, and sort the materials into groups based on patterns in their shared properties).
	2-PS1-2—**Analyze data obtained from testing different materials to determine which materials have the properties that are best suited for an intended purpose** (for example, test the strength, flexibility, hardness, texture, and absorbency of various materials, and use this qualitative information to decide which materials would work best for a given purpose).
	2-PS1-3—**Make observations to construct an evidence-based account of how an object made of a small set of pieces can be disassembled and made into a new object** (for example, observe as the same set of blocks or building bricks is taken apart and put back together—by the student or the teacher—to form various structures, and use these observations to defend the claim that an object made of a small set of pieces can be disassembled and made into a new object).
Score 2.0	**2-PS1-1**—The student will:
	• Recognize or recall specific vocabulary (for example, *classify, color, flexibility, hardness, material, observable property, pattern, property, shared property, states of matter, texture*).
	• Sort materials into teacher-provided groups based on their observable properties.
	2-PS1-2—The student will:
	• Recognize or recall specific vocabulary (for example, *absorbency, flexibility, flexible, hard, hardness, material, porous, property, purpose, rough, scratchy, smooth, soft, strength, strong, texture*).
	• Describe the properties of various materials (for example, strong, flexible, hard, soft, rough, scratchy, smooth, and porous).
	2-PS1-3—The student will:
	• Recognize or recall specific vocabulary (for example, *assemble, disassemble, evidence-based, form, observation, piece, reassemble*).
	• Describe an object as being made of smaller pieces (for example, describe a snap-cube structure as being made of individual pieces).

Conservation of Matter

	High School		
Score 4.0	In addition to score 3.0 performance, the student demonstrates in-depth inferences and applications that go beyond what was taught.		
	Score 3.5	*In addition to score 3.0 performance, partial success at score 4.0 content*	
Score 3.0	The student will: **HS-PS1-7—Use mathematical representations to support the claim that atoms, and therefore mass, are conserved during a chemical reaction** (for example, use mathematical ideas—not memorization or rote application of problem-solving techniques—to explain the proportional relationships between the masses of atoms in the reactants and the products of a chemical reaction as well as the translation of these relationships from the atomic to the macroscopic scale using the mole as a conversion).		
	Score 2.5	*No major errors or omissions regarding score 2.0 content, and partial success at score 3.0 content*	
Score 2.0	**HS-PS1-7**—The student will: • Recognize or recall specific vocabulary (for example, *atom, atomic mass, atomic scale, chemical reaction, conserve, conversion, macroscopic scale, mass, molar volume, mole, product, proportional, reactant, relationship, release of energy, translation*). • Describe the masses of atoms in reactants and products of a chemical reaction. • Convert masses of atoms between the atomic and macroscopic scale (for example, atomic mass to moles).		
	Score 1.5	*Partial success at score 2.0 content, and major errors or omissions regarding score 3.0 content*	
Score 1.0	With help, partial success at score 2.0 content and score 3.0 content		
	Score 0.5	*With help, partial success at score 2.0 content but not at score 3.0 content*	
Score 0.0	Even with help, no success		
	Middle School		
Score 3.0	The student will: **MS-PS1-5—Develop and use a model to describe how the total number of atoms does not change in a chemical reaction and thus mass is conserved** (for example, apply the law of conservation of matter to create physical models or drawings that represent atoms before and after a chemical reaction).		
Score 2.0	**MS-PS1-5**—The student will: • Recognize or recall specific vocabulary (for example, *atom, chemical reaction, conserve, law of conservation of matter, mass, molecule, property*). • Describe the basic nature of a chemical reaction. • Describe the atomic structure of a molecule.		
	Grade 5		
Score 3.0	The student will: **5-PS1-2—Measure and graph quantities to provide evidence that regardless of the type of change that occurs when heating, cooling, or mixing substances, the total weight of matter is conserved** (for example, weigh a substance before and after it goes through a phase change, dissolves, or mixes with another substance to form a new one, and then graph the results).		
Score 2.0	**5-PS1-2**—The student will: • Recognize or recall specific vocabulary (for example, *change, conservation of mass, conservation of matter, conserve, cool, dissolve, heat, matter, mix, phase change, quantity, scale, substance, weigh, weight*). • Name and describe the changes that occur when heating, cooling, or mixing substances. • Use scales to measure weight. • Plot numbers on a graph.		

Chemical Reactions

High School		
Score 4.0	In addition to score 3.0 performance, the student demonstrates in-depth inferences and applications that go beyond what was taught.	
	Score 3.5	*In addition to score 3.0 performance, partial success at score 4.0 content*
Score 3.0	The student will: **HS-PS1-2—Construct and revise an explanation for the outcome of a simple chemical reaction based on the outermost electron states of atoms, trends in the periodic table, and knowledge of the patterns of chemical properties** (for example, explain the reasoning behind reactions between main group elements such as sodium and chlorine, carbon and oxygen, or carbon and hydrogen). **HS-PS1-5—Apply scientific principles and evidence to provide an explanation about the effects of changing the temperature or concentration of the reacting particles on the rate at which a reaction occurs** (for example, use evidence from temperature, concentration, and rate data to explain qualitative relationships between rate and temperature in a simple reaction with two reactants, focusing on the number and energy of collisions between molecules). **HS-PS1-6—Refine the design of a chemical system by specifying a change in conditions that would produce increased amounts of products at equilibrium** (for example, apply Le Chatelier's principle to think of ways to increase product formation through the addition of reactants or removal of products).	
	Score 2.5	*No major errors or omissions regarding score 2.0 content, and partial success at score 3.0 content*
Score 2.0	**HS-PS1-2**—The student will: • Recognize or recall specific vocabulary (for example, *acid/base reaction, atom, atomic configuration, atomic reaction, carbon, chemical property, chemical properties of elements, chemical reaction rate, hydrogen, main group element, outcome, outermost electron state, pattern, periodic table, reaction, simple chemical reaction, sodium, trend*). • Describe the outermost electron states of atoms, trends in the periodic table, and patterns of chemical properties. • Describe the relationship between chemical reactions and outermost electron states of atoms, trends in the periodic table, and patterns of chemical properties. **HS-PS1-5**—The student will: • Recognize or recall specific vocabulary (for example, *accelerator, catalyst, collision, concentration, data, endothermic reaction, energy, exothermic reaction, molecule, oxidation-reduction, particle, properties of reactants, radical reaction, rate, react, reactant, reaction, recombination of chemical elements, simple reaction, temperature*). • Describe the effects of changing the temperature or concentration of the reacting particles on the rate at which a reaction occurs. **HS-PS1-6**—The student will: • Recognize or recall specific vocabulary (for example, *chemical reaction rate, chemical system, endothermic reaction, equilibrium, exothermic reaction, formation, Le Chatelier's principle, product, reactant*). • Describe the relationship between elements in a chemical system. • Describe how products reach equilibrium.	
	Score 1.5	*Partial success at score 2.0 content, and major errors or omissions regarding score 3.0 content*
Score 1.0	With help, partial success at score 2.0 content and score 3.0 content	
	Score 0.5	*With help, partial success at score 2.0 content but not at score 3.0 content*
Score 0.0	Even with help, no success	

Middle School	
Score 3.0	The student will: **MS-PS1-2—Analyze and interpret data on the properties of substances before and after the substances interact to determine if a chemical reaction has occurred** (for example, observe the density, melting point, boiling point, solubility, flammability, or odor of substances before and after they interact, and compare these observations). **MS-PS1-3—Gather and make sense of information to describe that synthetic materials come from natural resources and impact society** (for example, collect and evaluate qualitative information about natural resources that undergo a chemical process to form new medicines, foods, or alternative fuels). **MS-PS1-6—Undertake a design project to construct, test, and modify a device that either releases or absorbs thermal energy by chemical processes** (for example, create a device whose substances chemically react, and modify the type and concentration of those substances to control the transfer of energy into the environment).
Score 2.0	**MS-PS1-2—The student will:** • Recognize or recall specific vocabulary (for example, *boiling point, chemical compound, chemical element, chemical energy, chemical reaction, concentration of reactants, density, flammability, food oxidation, interact, melting point, metal reactivity, nonmetal reactivity, nonreactive gas, observation, odor, oxidation, property, reaction rate, rusting, solubility, substance, surface area of reactants*). • Describe signs or signals that indicate a chemical reaction. • Describe how a substance changes before and after a chemical reaction. **MS-PS1-3—The student will:** • Recognize or recall specific vocabulary (for example, *alternative fuel, chemical compound, chemical element, chemical process, impact, natural resource, society, synthetic material*). • Describe the chemical processes that convert natural resources to new materials. • Describe the impacts of synthetic materials on society. **MS-PS1-6—The student will:** • Recognize or recall specific vocabulary (for example, *absorb, chemical compound, chemical element, chemical energy, chemical process, chemical reaction, concentration, concentration of reactants, device, energy, environment, release, substance, thermal energy, transfer of energy*). • Describe chemical processes that release or absorb thermal energy.
Grade 5	
Score 3.0	The student will: **5-PS1-4—Conduct an investigation to determine whether the mixing of two or more substances results in new substances** (for example, observe the mixing of two or more substances and decide whether a chemical reaction has occurred).
Score 2.0	**5-PS1-4—The student will:** • Recognize or recall specific vocabulary (for example, *chemical reaction, mix, substance*). • Describe the signs or signals that indicate a chemical reaction.

Bonds

	High School
Score 4.0	In addition to score 3.0 performance, the student demonstrates in-depth inferences and applications that go beyond what was taught.
	Score 3.5 *In addition to score 3.0 performance, partial success at score 4.0 content*
Score 3.0	The student will: **HS-PS1-4—Develop a model to illustrate that the release or absorption of energy from a chemical reaction system depends upon the changes in total bond energy** (for example, create a molecular-level drawing or diagram of a reaction, a graph showing the relative energies of reactants and products, or a representation showing that energy is conserved to illustrate that a chemical reaction is a system that affects energy change).
	Score 2.5 *No major errors or omissions regarding score 2.0 content, and partial success at score 3.0 content*
Score 2.0	**HS-PS1-4—**The student will: • Recognize or recall specific vocabulary (for example, *absorption, bond, bond energy, change, chemical reaction, conserve, energy, molecular level, product, reactant, reaction, relative energy, release, system*). • Create diagrams of chemical reactions. • Describe changes in total bond energy during a chemical reaction.
	Score 1.5 *Partial success at score 2.0 content, and major errors or omissions regarding score 3.0 content*
Score 1.0	With help, partial success at score 2.0 content and score 3.0 content
	Score 0.5 *With help, partial success at score 2.0 content but not at score 3.0 content*
Score 0.0	Even with help, no success

Nuclear Processes

	High School
Score 4.0	In addition to score 3.0 performance, the student demonstrates in-depth inferences and applications that go beyond what was taught.
	Score 3.5 *In addition to score 3.0 performance, partial success at score 4.0 content*
Score 3.0	The student will: **HS-PS1-8—Develop models to illustrate the changes in the composition of the nucleus of the atom and the energy released during the processes of fission, fusion, and radioactive decay** (for example, create simple qualitative pictures or diagrams to show changes in the composition of the nucleus of the atom and the scale of energy released—relative to other kinds of transformations—during the processes of fission, fusion, and alpha, beta, and gamma radioactive decays).
	Score 2.5 *No major errors or omissions regarding score 2.0 content, and partial success at score 3.0 content*
Score 2.0	**HS-PS1-8—**The student will: • Recognize or recall specific vocabulary (for example, *alpha radioactive decay, atom, atomic bomb, beta radioactive decay, decay rate, Enrico Fermi, Ernest Rutherford, fission, fusion, gamma radioactive decay, hydrogen bomb, Lise Meitner, Marie Curie, nuclear force, nuclear mass, nuclear reaction, nuclear stability, nucleus, particle emission, Pierre Curie, radioactive decay, rate of nuclear decay, release, spontaneous nuclear reaction, transformation*). • Describe the processes of fission, fusion, and alpha, beta, and gamma radioactive decay.
	Score 1.5 *Partial success at score 2.0 content, and major errors or omissions regarding score 3.0 content*
Score 1.0	With help, partial success at score 2.0 content and score 3.0 content
	Score 0.5 *With help, partial success at score 2.0 content but not at score 3.0 content*
Score 0.0	Even with help, no success

Life Sciences

Growth and Development of Organisms

	Middle School	
Score 4.0	In addition to score 3.0 performance, the student demonstrates in-depth inferences and applications that go beyond what was taught.	
	Score 3.5	*In addition to score 3.0 performance, partial success at score 4.0 content*
Score 3.0	The student will: **MS-LS1-4—Use argument based on empirical evidence and scientific reasoning to support an explanation for how characteristic animal behaviors and specialized plant structures affect the probability of successful reproduction of animals and plants respectively** (for example, using empirical evidence and scientific reasoning, make and defend the claim that specific animal behaviors affect the probability of animal and plant reproduction [such as nest building to protect young from cold, herding to protect young from predators, transferring pollen or seeds to create conditions for seed germination, or animal vocalization and colorful plumage to attract mates for breeding] and that specific plant structures affect the probability of successful plant reproduction [such as bright flowers attracting butterflies that transfer pollen, flower nectar and odors attracting insects that transfer pollen, and hard shells on nuts that squirrels bury]). **MS-LS1-5—Construct a scientific explanation based on evidence for how environmental and genetic factors influence the growth of organisms** (for example, use evidence [such as drought decreasing plant growth, fertilizer increasing plant growth, different varieties of plant seeds growing at different rates in different conditions, and fish growing larger or smaller depending on habitat size] to explain how genetic factors and environmental factors [such as availability of food, light, space, and water] affect the growth of organisms).	
	Score 2.5	*No major errors or omissions regarding score 2.0 content, and partial success at score 3.0 content*
Score 2.0	**MS-LS1-4**—The student will: • Recognize or recall specific vocabulary (for example, *animal, animal behavior, attract, breed, characteristic, mate, nectar, plant, plant structure, pollen, probability, reproduction, reproductive capacity, reproductive system, specialized*). • Describe animal behaviors that affect the probability of successful reproduction. • Describe plant structures that affect the probability of successful reproduction. **MS-LS1-5**—The student will: • Recognize or recall specific vocabulary (for example, *characteristics of life, drought, environmental, factor, fertilizer, genetic, growth, organism, soil fertility*). • Describe environmental and genetic factors that influence the growth of organisms.	
	Score 1.5	*Partial success at score 2.0 content, and major errors or omissions regarding score 3.0 content*
Score 1.0	With help, partial success at score 2.0 content and score 3.0 content	
	Score 0.5	*With help, partial success at score 2.0 content but not at score 3.0 content*
Score 0.0	Even with help, no success	

continued →

	Grade 3
Score 3.0	The student will: **3-LS1-1—Develop models to describe that organisms have unique and diverse life cycles but all have in common birth, growth, reproduction, and death** (for example, create models of the life cycles of different organisms, and use them to explain that certain changes organisms go through during their lives form a common pattern).
Score 2.0	3-LS1-1—The student will: • Recognize or recall specific vocabulary (for example, *birth, death, growth, life cycle, organism, reproduction*). • Identify the stages of a life cycle.

	Grade 1
Score 3.0	The student will: **1-LS1-2—Read texts and use media to determine patterns in behavior of parents and offspring that help offspring survive** (for example, read grade-appropriate scientific texts and use other types of media to identify behavioral patterns of survival among parents and offspring, such as signals that offspring make [including crying, cheeping, and other vocalizations] and the responses of parents [including feeding, comforting, and protection]).
Score 2.0	1-LS1-2—The student will: • Recognize or recall specific vocabulary (for example, *behavior, behavior pattern, offspring, parent, response, shelter, signal, survive*). • Describe the ways animal parents help their offspring survive. • State factors that threaten or inhibit the survival of animals.

Matter and Energy in Organisms

	High School	
Score 4.0	In addition to score 3.0 performance, the student demonstrates in-depth inferences and applications that go beyond what was taught.	
	Score 3.5	*In addition to score 3.0 performance, partial success at score 4.0 content*
Score 3.0	The student will: **HS-LS1-5—Use a model to illustrate how photosynthesis transforms light energy into stored chemical energy** (for example, use diagrams, chemical equations, and conceptual models to show the inputs and outputs of matter and the transfer and transformation of energy in photosynthesis by plants and other photosynthesizing organisms). **HS-LS1-6—Construct and revise an explanation based on evidence for how carbon, hydrogen, and oxygen from sugar molecules may combine with other elements to form amino acids and/or other large carbon-based molecules** (for example, use evidence from models and simulations to support an explanation for how elements in sugar molecules combine with other elements to form amino acids or other large carbon-based molecules). **HS-LS1-7—Use a model to illustrate that cellular respiration is a chemical process whereby the bonds of food molecules and oxygen molecules are broken and the bonds in new compounds are formed resulting in a net transfer of energy** (for example, use a model to demonstrate a conceptual understanding of the inputs and outputs of the process of cellular respiration).	
	Score 2.5	*No major errors or omissions regarding score 2.0 content, and partial success at score 3.0 content*

Score 2.0	**HS-LS1-5**—The student will: • Recognize or recall specific vocabulary (for example, *chemical energy, convert, energy, input, light energy, matter, organism, output, photosynthesis, photosynthesizing organism, plant, stored energy, transfer, transform, transformation*). • Describe how plants use photosynthesis. • Describe the inputs and outputs of photosynthesis. **HS-LS1-6**—The student will: • Recognize or recall specific vocabulary (for example, *amino acid, amino acid sequence, biological molecule, carbon, carbon-based molecule, combine, element, hydrogen, molecule, oxygen, sugar*). • Describe how the body uses amino acids and other large, carbon-based molecules. **HS-LS1-7**—The student will: • Recognize or recall specific vocabulary (for example, *bond, cellular respiration, chemical process, compound, energy, food, form, input, molecule, net transfer, output, oxygen*). • Describe how organisms use cellular respiration. • Describe the inputs and outputs of cellular respiration.		
	Score 1.5	*Partial success at score 2.0 content, and major errors or omissions regarding score 3.0 content*	
Score 1.0	With help, partial success at score 2.0 content and score 3.0 content		
	Score 0.5	*With help, partial success at score 2.0 content but not at score 3.0 content*	
Score 0.0	Even with help, no success		

Middle School			
Score 3.0	The student will: **MS-LS1-6**—**Construct a scientific explanation based on evidence for the role of photosynthesis in the cycling of matter and flow of energy into and out of organisms** (for example, use evidence to explain the role of photosynthesis in cycles of matter and energy by tracing the movement of matter and the flow of energy within a photosynthetic system). **MS-LS1-7**—**Develop a model to describe how food is rearranged through chemical reactions forming new molecules that support growth and/or release energy as this matter moves through an organism** (for example, create a model and use it to explain that molecules are broken apart and put back together and that energy is released when organisms ingest food).		
Score 2.0	**MS-LS1-6**—The student will: • Recognize or recall specific vocabulary (for example, *cycle, energy, flow, matter, organism, photosynthesis, photosynthetic system, role*). • Describe the relationship between the process of photosynthesis and the cycling of matter and the flow of energy in organisms. **MS-LS1-7**—The student will: • Recognize or recall specific vocabulary (for example, *body, chemical reaction, energy, food, growth, ingest, Louis Pasteur, matter, molecule, organism, release, support*). • Describe how the body uses food.		

Grade 5			
Score 3.0	The student will: **5-PS3-1**—**Use models to describe that energy in animals' food (used for body repair, growth, motion, and to maintain body warmth) was once energy from the sun** (for example, use diagrams and flow charts to explain that the energy in animals' food originally came from the sun). **5-LS1-1**—**Support an argument that plants get the materials they need for growth chiefly from air and water** (for example, make and defend the claim that plant matter comes mostly from air and water, not soil).		

continued →

Score 2.0	5-PS3-1—The student will:
	• Recognize or recall specific vocabulary (for example, *animal, body repair, body warmth, energy, flow chart, food, growth, motion, store, sun, water*).
	• Describe why animals need food.
	• Describe how the sun's energy is stored in food.
	5-LS1-1—The student will:
	• Recognize or recall specific vocabulary (for example, *air, growth, material, photosynthetic plant, plant, plant matter, soil, water*).
	• Describe how plants get the materials they need for growth.
	• Describe the relationship between plants, air, water, and soil.

Grade 2	
Score 3.0	The student will:
	2-LS2-1—Plan and conduct an investigation to determine if plants need sunlight and water to grow (for example, plan and carry out an investigation—testing one variable at a time—to figure out if plants need sunlight and water to grow).
Score 2.0	**2-LS2-1**—The student will:
	• Recognize or recall specific vocabulary (for example, *grow, investigation, plant, sunlight, variable, water*).
	• Identify different things that help plants to grow.

Kindergarten	
Score 3.0	The student will:
	K-LS1-1—Use observations to describe patterns of what plants and animals (including humans) need to survive (for example, make observations of different ways in which plants and animals survive and identify patterns—such as animals needing food versus plants needing light, certain types of animals needing specific kinds of food, or all living things needing water).
Score 2.0	**K-LS1-1**—The student will:
	• Recognize or recall specific vocabulary (for example, *animal, food, human, light, living thing, pattern, plant, requirements for life, sunlight, survive, water*).
	• Identify different things that animals and plants need to survive (such as sunlight, water, and food).

Ecosystem Dynamics

High School	
Score 4.0	In addition to score 3.0 performance, the student demonstrates in-depth inferences and applications that go beyond what was taught.
	Score 3.5 *In addition to score 3.0 performance, partial success at score 4.0 content*
Score 3.0	The student will:
	HS-LS2-1—Use mathematical and/or computational representations to support explanations of factors that affect carrying capacity of ecosystems at different scales (for example, use quantitative analysis to compare the relationships among interdependent factors—such as boundaries, resources, climate, and competition—based on graphs, charts, histograms, or population changes gathered from simulations or historical data sets).

	HS-LS2-2—Use mathematical representations to support and revise explanations based on evidence about factors affecting biodiversity and populations in ecosystems of different scales (for example, use mathematical representations—such as finding the average, determining trends, and using graphical comparisons of multiple sets of teacher-provided data—to support and revise explanations about factors affecting biodiversity and populations in ecosystems).	
	HS-LS2-6—Evaluate the claims, evidence, and reasoning that the complex interactions in ecosystems maintain relatively consistent numbers and types of organisms in stable conditions, but changing conditions may result in a new ecosystem (for example, evaluate the evidence and reasoning behind the claim that in stable conditions, ecosystems maintain relatively consistent numbers and types of organisms, but that a shift in biological or physical conditions [such as moderate hunting or a seasonal flood] or an extreme change [such as volcanic eruption or sea-level rise] can result in a new ecosystem).	
	Score 2.5	*No major errors or omissions regarding score 2.0 content, and partial success at score 3.0 content*
Score 2.0	**HS-LS2-1**—The student will: • Recognize or recall specific vocabulary (for example, *boundary, carrying capacity, climate, competition, data set, ecosystem, factor, graph, histogram, interdependent, population, quantitative analysis, relationship, resource, scale, simulation*). • Describe how various factors affect the carrying capacity of ecosystems (for example, boundaries, resources, climate, and competition). **HS-LS2-2**—The student will: • Recognize or recall specific vocabulary (for example, *average, biodiversity, data set, ecosystem, equilibrium, factor, population, scale, trend*). • Describe how various factors affect the biodiversity and populations of ecosystems. **HS-LS2-6**—The student will: • Recognize or recall specific vocabulary (for example, *biological, change, condition, consistent, ecosystem, extreme, interaction, organism, physical, shift, stable, transition, volcanic eruption*). • Describe the effects of transitions in ecosystems.	
	Score 1.5	*Partial success at score 2.0 content, and major errors or omissions regarding score 3.0 content*
Score 1.0	With help, partial success at score 2.0 content and score 3.0 content	
	Score 0.5	*With help, partial success at score 2.0 content but not at score 3.0 content*
Score 0.0	Even with help, no success	
	Middle School	
Score 3.0	The student will: **MS-LS2-1**—Analyze and interpret data to provide evidence for the effects of resource availability on organisms and populations of organisms in an ecosystem (for example, analyze and interpret data to support claims about the cause and effect relationships between resources, growth of individual organisms, and the numbers of organisms in an ecosystem during periods of abundant and scarce resources). **MS-LS2-4**—Construct an argument supported by empirical evidence that changes to physical or biological components of an ecosystem affect populations (for example, recognize patterns in data, make warranted inferences about changes in populations, and evaluate empirical evidence about ecosystem changes to make and defend the claim that biological or physical changes to an ecosystem can affect populations).	

continued →

Score 2.0	MS-LS2-1—The student will:
	• Recognize or recall specific vocabulary (for example, *abundant*, *cause*, *ecosystem*, *effect*, *environmental condition*, *growth*, *organism*, *population*, *relationship*, *resource*, *resource availability*, *scarce*).
	• Describe the effects of varying levels of resource availability on organisms and populations.
	MS-LS2-4—The student will:
	• Recognize or recall specific vocabulary (for example, *biological*, *change*, *component*, *ecosystem*, *environmental change*, *physical*, *population*, *population density*, *relationship*).
	• Describe the relationship between populations and the physical and biological components of an ecosystem.
Grade 2	
Score 3.0	The student will:
	2-LS4-1—Make observations of plants and animals to compare the diversity of life in different habitats (for example, observe various plants and animals—firsthand or from media—and use these observations to make comparisons between the different kinds of living things in different habitats on land and in water).
Score 2.0	2-LS4-1—The student will:
	• Recognize or recall specific vocabulary (for example, *animal*, *compare*, *comparison*, *diversity of life*, *habitat*, *land*, *living thing*, *observation*, *plant*, *water*).
	• Describe different types of animals and different types of habitats.

Interdependent Relationships in Ecosystems

High School	
Score 4.0	In addition to score 3.0 performance, the student demonstrates in-depth inferences and applications that go beyond what was taught.
	Score 3.5 — *In addition to score 3.0 performance, partial success at score 4.0 content*
Score 3.0	The student will:
	HS-LS2-8—Evaluate the evidence for the role of group behavior on individual and species' chances to survive and reproduce (for example, review and evaluate information to distinguish between group behavior, such as flocking, schooling, and herding; cooperative behavior, such as hunting, migrating, and swarming; and individual behavior to identify evidence supporting the outcomes of group behavior and to develop logical and reasonable arguments based on this evidence).
	Score 2.5 — *No major errors or omissions regarding score 2.0 content, and partial success at score 3.0 content*
Score 2.0	HS-LS2-8—The student will:
	• Recognize or recall specific vocabulary (for example, *cooperative behavior*, *group behavior*, *individual behavior*, *outcome*, *reproduce*, *species*, *survive*).
	• Describe the relationship between group behavior and individual survival.
	Score 1.5 — *Partial success at score 2.0 content, and major errors or omissions regarding score 3.0 content*
Score 1.0	With help, partial success at score 2.0 content and score 3.0 content
	Score 0.5 — *With help, partial success at score 2.0 content but not at score 3.0 content*
Score 0.0	Even with help, no success
Middle School	
Score 3.0	The student will:
	MS-LS2-2—Construct an explanation that predicts patterns of interactions among organisms across multiple ecosystems (for example, explain how one might predict consistent patterns of interactions—such as competitive, predatory, and mutually beneficial—in different ecosystems in terms of the relationships among and between organisms and abiotic components of an ecosystem).

Score 2.0	MS-LS2-2—The student will: • Recognize or recall specific vocabulary (for example, *abiotic, competitive, component, ecological role, ecosystem, host, infection, interaction, mutualism, mutually beneficial, organism, parasite, predatory, relationship*). • Describe patterns of interactions among organisms across multiple ecosystems.
Grade 3	
Score 3.0	The student will: **3-LS2-1—Construct an argument that some animals form groups that help members survive** (for example, make and defend the claim that being part of a group helps animals obtain food, defend themselves, and cope with changes).
Score 2.0	**3-LS2-1**—The student will: • Recognize or recall specific vocabulary (for example, *animal, cope, defend, food, group, member, survive*). • Identify animals that form groups to survive. • Describe benefits of forming groups.
Grade 2	
Score 3.0	The student will: **2-LS2-2—Develop a simple model that mimics the function of an animal in dispersing seeds or pollinating plants** (for example, create a sketch, drawing, or physical model that demonstrates how animals move seeds around or pollinate plants).
Score 2.0	**2-LS2-2**—The student will: • Recognize or recall specific vocabulary (for example, *animal, disperse, function, plant, pollinate, seed*). • Identify animals that disperse seeds or pollinate plants. • Describe how animals disperse seeds or pollinate plants.

Matter and Energy in Ecosystems

	High School	
Score 4.0	In addition to score 3.0 performance, the student demonstrates in-depth inferences and applications that go beyond what was taught.	
	Score 3.5	*In addition to score 3.0 performance, partial success at score 4.0 content*
Score 3.0	The student will: **HS-LS2-3—Construct and revise an explanation based on evidence for the cycling of matter and flow of energy in aerobic and anaerobic conditions** (for example, use evidence to create and evaluate an explanation of the role of aerobic and anaerobic respiration in different environments). **HS-LS2-4—Use mathematical representations to support claims for the cycling of matter and flow of energy among organisms in an ecosystem** (for example, use a mathematical model of stored energy in biomass to describe the transfer of energy from one trophic level to another and to explain that matter—particularly atoms and molecules such as carbon, oxygen, hydrogen, and nitrogen—and energy are conserved as matter cycles and energy flows through an ecosystem). **HS-LS2-5—Develop a model to illustrate the role of photosynthesis and cellular respiration in the cycling of carbon among the biosphere, atmosphere, hydrosphere, and geosphere** (for example, create a simulation or mathematical model to show how photosynthesis and cellular respiration are involved in the cycling of carbon among the biosphere, atmosphere, hydrosphere, and geosphere).	
	Score 2.5	*No major errors or omissions regarding score 2.0 content, and partial success at score 3.0 content*

continued →

Score 2.0	HS-LS2-3—The student will:
	• Recognize or recall specific vocabulary (for example, *aerobic, anaerobic, cycle, energy, environment, flow, matter, respiration, role*).
	• Describe how matter cycles and energy flows in aerobic and anaerobic conditions.
	HS-LS2-4—The student will:
	• Recognize or recall specific vocabulary (for example, *atom, biomass, carbon, conserve, cycle, ecosystem, energy, flow, hydrogen, matter, molecule, nitrogen, organism, oxygen, store, transfer, trophic level*).
	• Describe the matter cycles and energy flows among organisms in an ecosystem.
	HS-LS2-5—The student will:
	• Recognize or recall specific vocabulary (for example, *atmosphere, biosphere, carbon cycle, cellular respiration, geosphere, hydrosphere, photosynthesis*).
	• State accurate information about photosynthesis, cellular respiration, and the carbon cycle.
	Score 1.5 *Partial success at score 2.0 content, and major errors or omissions regarding score 3.0 content*
Score 1.0	With help, partial success at score 2.0 content and score 3.0 content
	Score 0.5 *With help, partial success at score 2.0 content but not at score 3.0 content*
Score 0.0	Even with help, no success
Middle School	
Score 3.0	The student will:
	MS-LS2-3—Develop a model to describe the cycling of matter and flow of energy among living and nonliving parts of an ecosystem (for example, create a model and use it to describe the conservation of matter and the flow of energy in and out of various ecosystems as well as to define the boundaries of the system).
Score 2.0	MS-LS2-3—The student will:
	• Recognize or recall specific vocabulary (for example, *boundary, conservation of matter, cycle, ecosystem, energy, flow, living, matter, nonliving, organism, system*).
	• State accurate information about the cycling of matter and flow of energy in organisms and ecosystems.
Grade 5	
Score 3.0	The student will:
	5-LS2-1—Develop a model to describe the movement of matter among plants, animals, decomposers, and the environment (for example, create a model that shows the cycle of organisms changing matter that is not food [such as air, water, or decomposed materials in soil] into matter that is food, animals eating plants [or eating the animals that eat plants] for food, and then all organisms releasing waste matter [gas, liquid, or solid] back into the environment).
Score 2.0	5-LS2-1—The student will:
	• Recognize or recall specific vocabulary (for example, *air, animal, cycle, decompose, decomposer, environment, food, gas, liquid, matter, organism, plant, soil, solid, waste matter, water*).
	• Describe different ways in which plants, animals, decomposers, and the environment use matter.

Humans, Biodiversity, and Ecosystems

	High School	
Score 4.0	In addition to score 3.0 performance, the student demonstrates in-depth inferences and applications that go beyond what was taught.	
	Score 3.5	*In addition to score 3.0 performance, partial success at score 4.0 content*
Score 3.0	The student will: **HS-LS2-7—Design, evaluate, and refine a solution for reducing the impacts of human activities on the environment and biodiversity** (for example, use scientific knowledge, student-generated sources of evidence, prioritized criteria, and tradeoff considerations to design, evaluate, and refine a solution for reducing the environmental impact of human activities, such as urbanization, construction of dams, and dissemination of invasive species). **HS-LS4-6—Create or revise a simulation to test a solution to mitigate adverse impacts of human activity on biodiversity** (for example, design a solution for a proposed problem related to threatened or endangered species or to genetic variation of organisms for multiple species, and create and revise a simulation to test that solution).	
	Score 2.5	*No major errors or omissions regarding score 2.0 content, and partial success at score 3.0 content*
Score 2.0	**HS-LS2-7**—The student will: • Recognize or recall specific vocabulary (for example, *biodiversity, dam, dissemination, environment, environmental impact, human activity, impact, invasive species, reduce, social, technological, tradeoff, urbanization*). • Describe how technological or social methods have attempted to reduce the impact of human activities. **HS-LS4-6**—The student will: • Recognize or recall specific vocabulary (for example, *adverse, biodiversity, endangered species, genetic variation, human activity, human modification of ecosystems, impact, organism, species, threatened species*). • Describe ways in which human activity has an adverse impact on biodiversity.	
	Score 1.5	*Partial success at score 2.0 content, and major errors or omissions regarding score 3.0 content*
Score 1.0	With help, partial success at score 2.0 content and score 3.0 content	
	Score 0.5	*With help, partial success at score 2.0 content but not at score 3.0 content*
Score 0.0	Even with help, no success	
	Middle School	
Score 3.0	The student will: **MS-LS2-5—Evaluate competing design solutions for maintaining biodiversity and ecosystem services** (for example, based on scientific, economic, and social constraints, evaluate competing design solutions for maintaining biodiversity and ecosystem services, such as water purification, nutrient recycling, and soil erosion prevention).	
Score 2.0	**MS-LS2-5**—The student will: • Recognize or recall specific vocabulary (for example, *biodiversity, economic constraint, ecosystem, nutrient recycling, prevention, scientific constraint, service, social constraint, soil erosion, water purification*). • Describe the evaluation criteria used to evaluate design solutions. • Summarize competing design solutions for maintaining biodiversity and ecosystem services.	

Structure and Function

High School	
Score 4.0	In addition to score 3.0 performance, the student demonstrates in-depth inferences and applications that go beyond what was taught.
	Score 3.5 *In addition to score 3.0 performance, partial success at score 4.0 content*
Score 3.0	The student will: **HS-LS1-2—Develop and use a model to illustrate the hierarchical organization of interacting systems that provide specific functions within multicellular organisms** (for example, create a model and use it to explain the hierarchical organization of interacting systems [such as an artery depending on the proper function of elastic tissue and smooth muscle to regulate and deliver the proper amount of blood within the circulatory system] that provide specific functions within multicellular organisms at the system level [such as nutrient uptake, water delivery, and organism movement in response to neural stimuli]). **HS-LS1-3—Plan and conduct an investigation to provide evidence that feedback mechanisms maintain homeostasis** (for example, investigate feedback mechanisms—such as heart rate response to exercise, stomate response to moisture and temperature, and root development in response to water levels—to demonstrate that these mechanisms maintain homeostasis).
	Score 2.5 *No major errors or omissions regarding score 2.0 content, and partial success at score 3.0 content*
Score 2.0	**HS-LS1-2**—The student will: • Recognize or recall specific vocabulary (for example, *artery, blood, circulatory system, function, hierarchical organization, interact, movement, multicellular, muscle, neural, nutrient uptake, organism, regulate, response, stimulus, system, tissue, water delivery*). • Describe how various systems provide specific functions within multicellular organisms. **HS-LS1-3**—The student will: • Recognize or recall specific vocabulary (for example, *enzyme, exercise, feedback mechanism, heart rate, homeostasis, moisture, response, root development, stomate, temperature, water*). • Describe how various feedback mechanisms maintain homeostasis.
	Score 1.5 *Partial success at score 2.0 content, and major errors or omissions regarding score 3.0 content*
Score 1.0	With help, partial success at score 2.0 content and score 3.0 content
	Score 0.5 *With help, partial success at score 2.0 content but not at score 3.0 content*
Score 0.0	Even with help, no success
Middle School	
Score 3.0	The student will: **MS-LS1-3—Use argument supported by evidence for how the body is a system of interacting subsystems composed of groups of cells** (for example, make and defend the claim that the body is a system of interacting subsystems composed of groups of cells—such as the circulatory, excretory, digestive, respiratory, muscular, and nervous systems—using information about the interaction of subsystems within a system and the normal function of those systems).
Score 2.0	**MS-LS1-3**—The student will: • Recognize or recall specific vocabulary (for example, *body, cell, circulatory system, digestive system, excretory system, function, group, interact, interaction, internal structure, life-sustaining function, muscular system, nervous system, organ system, reproductive system, respiratory system, specialized organ, specialized tissue, subsystem, system, system failure*). • Summarize the function of various subsystems in the body system (such as the circulatory, excretory, digestive, respiratory, muscular, and nervous system). • Describe the relationship between different subsystems of the body system.

Grade 4	
Score 3.0	The student will: **4-LS1-1—Construct an argument that plants and animals have internal and external structures that function to support survival, growth, behavior, and reproduction** (for example, make and defend the claim that plants and animals have external and internal structures—such as thorns, stems, roots, colored petals, hearts, stomachs, lungs, brains, skin, and other macroscopic structures—that help them survive, grow, and reproduce).
Score 2.0	**4-LS1-1**—The student will: • Recognize or recall specific vocabulary (for example, *animal, behavior, external structure, factor, growth, internal structure, macroscopic, organ, plant, reproduction, root, survival*). • Describe the key parts of various external and internal structures in plants and animals. • State factors that threaten or inhibit the survival, growth, and reproduction of animals.
Grade 1	
Score 3.0	The student will: **1-LS1-1—Use materials to design a solution to a human problem by mimicking how plants and/or animals use their external parts to help them survive, grow, and meet their needs** (for example, figure out a solution to a human problem based on plant and animal methods of survival—such as designing clothing or equipment to protect bicyclists by mimicking turtle shells, acorn shells, and animal scales; creating stabilizing structures by mimicking animal tails and roots on plants; fending off predators by mimicking thorns on branches and animal quills; and detecting predators by mimicking eyes and ears—and use teacher-provided materials to construct the design).
Score 2.0	**1-LS1-1**—The student will: • Recognize or recall specific vocabulary (for example, *animal, external, feature, grow, mimic, need, predator, survival, survive*). • Describe external parts that plants or animals use to survive or grow.

Information Processing

Middle School		
Score 4.0	In addition to score 3.0 performance, the student demonstrates in-depth inferences and applications that go beyond what was taught.	
	Score 3.5	*In addition to score 3.0 performance, partial success at score 4.0 content*
Score 3.0	The student will: **MS-LS1-8—Gather and synthesize information that sensory receptors respond to stimuli by sending messages to the brain for immediate behavior or storage as memories** (for example, research and summarize the basic process of sensory receptors responding to stimuli by sending messages to the brain for immediate behavior or storage as memories).	
	Score 2.5	*No major errors or omissions regarding score 2.0 content, and partial success at score 3.0 content*
Score 2.0	**MS-LS1-8**—The student will: • Recognize or recall specific vocabulary (for example, *behavior, behavioral response to stimuli, brain, immediate, memory, receptor, respond, sensory receptor, stimulus, storage*). • Identify various sensory receptors in the body. • Describe various ways the body can use information from sensory receptors.	
	Score 1.5	*Partial success at score 2.0 content, and major errors or omissions regarding score 3.0 content*
Score 1.0	With help, partial success at score 2.0 content and score 3.0 content	
	Score 0.5	*With help, partial success at score 2.0 content but not at score 3.0 content*
Score 0.0	Even with help, no success	

continued →

Grade 4	
Score 3.0	The student will: **4-LS1-2—Use a model to describe that animals receive different types of information through their senses, process the information in their brain, and respond to the information in different ways** (for example, create a model that explains the basic systems of information transfer that allow animals to use their perceptions and memories to guide their actions).
Score 2.0	**4-LS1-2—**The student will: • Recognize or recall specific vocabulary (for example, *action, animal, brain, information, memory, perception, respond, sense, sensory receptor, system, transfer*). • Describe the types of information animals receive through their senses. • Describe ways animals respond to information received through their senses.

Cell Theory

High School	
Score 4.0	In addition to score 3.0 performance, the student demonstrates in-depth inferences and applications that go beyond what was taught.
	Score 3.5 *In addition to score 3.0 performance, partial success at score 4.0 content*
Score 3.0	The student will: **HS-LS1-1—Construct an explanation based on evidence for how the structure of DNA determines the structure of proteins which carry out the essential functions of life through systems of specialized cells** (for example, use evidence to explain how the structure of DNA determines the structure of the proteins that carry out the essential functions of life through systems of specialized cells). **HS-LS1-4—Use a model to illustrate the role of cellular division (mitosis) and differentiation in producing and maintaining complex organisms** (for example, use a model to explain the role of mitosis and cellular differentiation in producing and maintaining complex organisms).
	Score 2.5 *No major errors or omissions regarding score 2.0 content, and partial success at score 3.0 content*
Score 2.0	**HS-LS1-1—**The student will: • Recognize or recall specific vocabulary (for example, *cell, DNA, essential, life function, protein, specialized, structure, system*). • Describe the relationship between the structure of DNA and the structure of proteins. **HS-LS1-4—**The student will: • Recognize or recall specific vocabulary (for example, *cellular communication, cellular differentiation, cellular division, maintain, mitosis, organism, produce*). • Summarize the process of cellular division (mitosis).
	Score 1.5 *Partial success at score 2.0 content, and major errors or omissions regarding score 3.0 content*
Score 1.0	With help, partial success at score 2.0 content and score 3.0 content
	Score 0.5 *With help, partial success at score 2.0 content but not at score 3.0 content*
Score 0.0	Even with help, no success

Middle School	
Score 3.0	The student will: **MS-LS1-1—Conduct an investigation to provide evidence that living things are made of cells; either one cell or many different numbers and types of cells** (for example, collect evidence that shows that living things differ from nonliving things because they are made of one or many varied cells). **MS-LS1-2—Develop and use a model to describe the function of a cell as a whole and ways parts of cells contribute to the function** (for example, create a model of a cell, and use it to explain how it functions as a whole system).
Score 2.0	**MS-LS1-1**—The student will: • Recognize or recall specific vocabulary (for example, *cell, fundamental unit of life, living, living thing, multicellular organism, nonliving, organism, unicellular organism, varied*). • Describe things that are made up of cells (living things) and things that are not made up of cells (nonliving things). **MS-LS1-2**—The student will: • Recognize or recall specific vocabulary (for example, *cell, cell function, cell growth, cell membrane, cell nucleus, cell organelle, cell wall, cellular energy conversion, cellular regulation, cellular response, cellular waste disposal, chloroplast, cytoplasm, egg cell, function, fundamental unit of life, Golgi apparatus, mitochondria, nucleated cell, nucleus, specialized cell, system, transport of cell material, vacuole*). • Describe the primary role of parts of the cell (for example, the nucleus, chloroplast, mitochondria, cell membrane, and cell wall).

Inheritance of Traits

High School		
Score 4.0	In addition to score 3.0 performance, the student demonstrates in-depth inferences and applications that go beyond what was taught.	
	Score 3.5	*In addition to score 3.0 performance, partial success at score 4.0 content*
Score 3.0	The student will: **HS-LS3-1—Ask questions to clarify relationships about the role of DNA and chromosomes in coding the instructions for characteristic traits passed from parents to offspring** (for example, formulate, refine, and evaluate empirically testable questions that arise from examining a model or theory to clarify the relationship between DNA and chromosomes and to help understand their respective functions).	
	Score 2.5	*No major errors or omissions regarding score 2.0 content, and partial success at score 3.0 content*
Score 2.0	**HS-LS3-1**—The student will: • Recognize or recall specific vocabulary (for example, *characteristic, chromosome, chromosome pair, code, DNA, function, instruction, offspring, parent, relationship, trait*). • Describe the functions of DNA and chromosomes. • Describe the relationships between DNA and chromosomes.	
	Score 1.5	*Partial success at score 2.0 content, and major errors or omissions regarding score 3.0 content*
Score 1.0	With help, partial success at score 2.0 content and score 3.0 content	
	Score 0.5	*With help, partial success at score 2.0 content but not at score 3.0 content*
Score 0.0	Even with help, no success	

continued →

Middle School	
Score 3.0	The student will: **MS-LS3-2—Develop and use a model to describe why asexual reproduction results in offspring with identical genetic information and sexual reproduction results in offspring with genetic variation** (for example, create and use models such as Punnett squares, diagrams, and simulations to describe the cause and effect relationship of gene transmission from parent(s) to offspring and the resulting genetic variation).
Score 2.0	MS-LS3-2—The student will: • Recognize or recall specific vocabulary (for example, *asexual reproduction, cause, effect, gene transmission, genetic, genetic variation, genotype, identical, offspring, parent, Punnett square, relationship, sexual reproduction, transmission*). • Describe sexual and asexual reproduction. • Use Punnett squares or other representations to describe possible genotype outcomes.
Grade 3	
Score 3.0	The student will: **3-LS3-1—Analyze and interpret data to provide evidence that plants and animals have traits inherited from parents and that variation of these traits exists in a group of similar organisms** (for example, analyze data and identify patterns in the similarities and differences in traits shared among siblings or between offspring and their parents—particularly of nonhuman organisms—to show that traits are inherited from parents and varied within a group of similar organisms).
Score 2.0	3-LS3-1—The student will: • Recognize or recall specific vocabulary (for example, *animal, difference, group, inherit, inherited characteristic, nonhuman, offspring, organism, parent, plant, sense, sibling, similar, trait, variation*). • Describe traits inherited from parents. • Describe similarities and differences in traits among siblings or between parents and offspring.
Grade 1	
Score 3.0	The student will: **1-LS3-1—Make observations to construct an evidence-based account that young plants and animals are like, but not exactly like, their parents** (for example, observe plants and animals that show evidence of inheritance—such as leaves from the same kind of plant that are the same shape but different in size or a puppy that looks similar to its parents—and use these observations to support the claim that young plants and animals are similar but not identical to their parents).
Score 2.0	1-LS3-1—The student will: • Recognize or recall specific vocabulary (for example, *animal, appearance, behavior, identical, inheritance, observation, offspring, parent, parent/offspring similarity, plant, similar*). • Describe the behavior and appearance of parents and offspring.

Variation of Traits

High School		
Score 4.0	In addition to score 3.0 performance, the student demonstrates in-depth inferences and applications that go beyond what was taught.	
	Score 3.5	*In addition to score 3.0 performance, partial success at score 4.0 content*

Score 3.0	The student will:
	HS-LS3-2—Make and defend a claim based on evidence that inheritable genetic variations may result from: (1) new genetic combinations through meiosis, (2) viable errors occurring during replication, and/or (3) mutations caused by environmental factors (for example, use data to make and defend claims about the different ways in which genetic variation occurs, excluding information about specific steps in the process).
	HS-LS3-3—Apply concepts of statistics and probability to explain the variation and distribution of expressed traits in a population (for example, use mathematics to describe the probability of traits as it relates to genetic and environmental factors in the expression of traits).

	Score 2.5	*No major errors or omissions regarding score 2.0 content, and partial success at score 3.0 content*

Score 2.0	**HS-LS3-2—The student will:**
	• Recognize or recall specific vocabulary (for example, *combination, environmental factor, error, gene, genetic, genetic variation, inheritable, meiosis, mutation, replication*).
	• Describe the ways in which inheritable genetic variations can develop (such as through meiosis, replication errors, or mutations).
	HS-LS3-3—The student will:
	• Recognize or recall specific vocabulary (for example, *distribution, environmental, expression, factor, genetic, population, probability, selective gene expression, statistics, trait, variation*).
	• Describe the variation and distribution of expressed traits in a population (for example, use a distribution curve to describe a population).

	Score 1.5	*Partial success at score 2.0 content, and major errors or omissions regarding score 3.0 content*

Score 1.0	With help, partial success at score 2.0 content and score 3.0 content

	Score 0.5	*With help, partial success at score 2.0 content but not at score 3.0 content*

Score 0.0	Even with help, no success

Middle School

Score 3.0	The student will:
	MS-LS3-1—Develop and use a model to describe why structural changes to genes (mutations) located on chromosomes may affect proteins and may result in harmful, beneficial, or neutral effects to the structure and function of the organism (for example, create and use a model to explain that general changes in genetic material may result in the creation of different proteins, which can affect the structure and function of an organism, thereby changing its traits).

Score 2.0	**MS-LS3-1—The student will:**
	• Recognize or recall specific vocabulary (for example, *beneficial, change, chromosome, function, gene, genetic material, harmful, mutation, neutral, organism, protein, structure, trait*).
	• Describe harmful, beneficial, and neutral effects of mutations.
	• Describe the relationship between genes, chromosomes, and proteins.

Grade 3

Score 3.0	The student will:
	3-LS3-2—Use evidence to support the explanation that traits can be influenced by the environment (for example, make and defend the claim that the environment can influence the traits of organisms—such as the lack of growth of plants due to insufficient water or the weight gain of a pet dog due to too much food and too little exercise).

Score 2.0	**3-LS3-2—The student will:**
	• Recognize or recall specific vocabulary (for example, *adaptation, difference, environment, individual difference, influence, organism, similarity, trait*).
	• Describe how traits can be influenced by the environment.
	• Describe how organisms have adapted to particular environments.

Adaptation

High School	
Score 4.0	In addition to score 3.0 performance, the student demonstrates in-depth inferences and applications that go beyond what was taught.
	Score 3.5 — *In addition to score 3.0 performance, partial success at score 4.0 content*
Score 3.0	The student will: **HS-LS4-4—Construct an explanation based on evidence for how natural selection leads to adaptation of populations** (for example, use data to provide evidence for how specific biotic and abiotic differences in ecosystems—such as ranges of seasonal temperature, long-term climate change, soil acidity, access to light, geographic barriers, or evolution of other organisms—contribute to a change in gene frequency over time, leading to the adaptation of populations). **HS-LS4-5—Evaluate the evidence supporting claims that changes in environmental conditions may result in: (1) increases in the number of individuals of some species, (2) the emergence of new species over time, and (3) the extinction of other species** (for example, evaluate the validity and reliability of the claim that changes to the environment—such as deforestation, fishing, the application of fertilizers, drought, flooding, and the rate of change to the environment—affect the distribution or disappearance of traits in species).
	Score 2.5 — *No major errors or omissions regarding score 2.0 content, and partial success at score 3.0 content*
Score 2.0	**HS-LS4-4—**The student will: • Recognize or recall specific vocabulary (for example, *adaptation, barrier, climate change, ecosystem, evolution, frequency, gene, geographic, light, natural selection, organism, population, soil acidity, temperature*). • Describe the relationship between natural selection and adaptation of populations. • Describe how differences in ecosystems can contribute to natural selection over time. **HS-LS4-5—**The student will: • Recognize or recall specific vocabulary (for example, *change, condition, deforestation, disappearance, distribution, diverge, drought, emergence, environment, environmental, extinction, fertilizer, fishing, flood, increase, rate of change, species, trait*). • Describe how environmental conditions can change over time. • Describe the relationship between environmental conditions and the distribution or disappearance of traits in a species.
	Score 1.5 — *Partial success at score 2.0 content, and major errors or omissions regarding score 3.0 content*
Score 1.0	With help, partial success at score 2.0 content and score 3.0 content
	Score 0.5 — *With help, partial success at score 2.0 content but not at score 3.0 content*
Score 0.0	Even with help, no success
Middle School	
Score 3.0	The student will: **MS-LS4-6—Use mathematical representations to support explanations of how natural selection may lead to increases and decreases of specific traits in populations over time** (for example, use mathematical models, probability statements, and proportional reasoning to support explanations of trends in changes to populations over time).
Score 2.0	**MS-LS4-6—**The student will: • Recognize or recall specific vocabulary (for example, *acquired trait, adaptive characteristic, behavioral change, decrease, emergence of life forms, increase, life form change, natural selection, population, probability, proportional, trait, trend*). • Describe the relationship between natural selection and trends in population traits over time.

Grade 3	
Score 3.0	The student will: **3-LS4-3—Construct an argument with evidence that in a particular habitat some organisms can survive well, some survive less well, and some cannot survive at all** (for example, use the needs and characteristics of organisms and habitats to defend the claim that in a particular habitat, some organisms survive well and some do not, and that the organisms and their habitat make up a system in which the parts depend on each other). **3-LS4-4—Make a claim about the merit of a solution to a problem caused when the environment changes and the types of plants and animals that live there may change** (for example, evaluate a solution to a problem caused by an environmental change—such as changes in land, water distribution, temperature, food, and other organisms—and give an opinion about the effectiveness of this solution).
Score 2.0	**3-LS4-3**—The student will: • Recognize or recall specific vocabulary (for example, *characteristic, depend, habitat, need, organism, survival of organisms, survive, system*). • Describe characteristic habitats for a variety of organisms. • Describe how traits can be advantageous in certain habitats and disadvantageous in others. **3-LS4-4**—The student will: • Recognize or recall specific vocabulary (for example, *animal, beneficial change, change, detrimental change, environment, food, land characteristic, organism, plant, temperature, water distribution*). • Describe changes that can happen to the environment. • Describe possible solutions to a problem caused by environmental change. • Describe the effects of environmental change on plants and animals.

Natural Selection

High School		
Score 4.0	In addition to score 3.0 performance, the student demonstrates in-depth inferences and applications that go beyond what was taught.	
	Score 3.5	*In addition to score 3.0 performance, partial success at score 4.0 content*
Score 3.0	The student will: **HS-LS4-2—Construct an explanation based on evidence that the process of evolution primarily results from four factors: (1) the potential for a species to increase in number, (2) the heritable genetic variation of individuals in a species due to mutation and sexual reproduction, (3) competition for limited resources, and (4) the proliferation of those organisms that are better able to survive and reproduce in the environment** (for example, use simple distribution graphs and proportional reasoning to explain the influence of each of the four factors on the number, behaviors, morphology, or physiology of organisms, particularly in terms of the ability of organisms to compete for limited resources and the subsequent survival of individuals and adaptation of the species). **HS-LS4-3—Apply concepts of statistics and probability to support explanations that organisms with an advantageous heritable trait tend to increase in proportion to organisms lacking this trait** (for example, use basic statistical and graphical analysis to analyze shifts in the numerical distribution of traits, and use these shifts as evidence to support the claim that organisms with an advantageous heritable trait tend to increase in proportion to organisms lacking this trait).	
	Score 2.5	*No major errors or omissions regarding score 2.0 content, and partial success at score 3.0 content*

continued →

Score 2.0	**HS-LS4-2**—The student will:
	• Recognize or recall specific vocabulary (for example, *adaptation, behavior, Charles Darwin, competition, environment, evolution, factor, genetic variation, heritable, influence, limited, morphology, mutation, organism, physiology, potential, proliferation, reproduce, resource, sexual reproduction, species, survive*).
	• Describe each of the four factors that are related to the process of evolution.
	HS-LS4-3—The student will:
	• Recognize or recall specific vocabulary (for example, *advantageous, distribution, heritable, increase, organism, proportional, reproductive value of traits, shift, survival, survival value of traits, trait*).
	• Demonstrate basic statistical and graphical analysis.
	• Describe the relationship between advantageous heritable traits and survival of organisms.

	Score 1.5	*Partial success at score 2.0 content, and major errors or omissions regarding score 3.0 content*
Score 1.0	With help, partial success at score 2.0 content and score 3.0 content	
	Score 0.5	*With help, partial success at score 2.0 content but not at score 3.0 content*
Score 0.0	Even with help, no success	

Middle School	
Score 3.0	The student will:
	MS-LS4-4—**Construct an explanation based on evidence that describes how genetic variations of traits in a population increase some individuals' probability of surviving and reproducing in a specific environment** (for example, use simple probability statements and proportional reasoning to defend the claim that genetic variations of traits in a population increase some individuals' probability of surviving and reproducing).
	MS-LS4-5—**Gather and synthesize information about the technologies that have changed the way humans influence the inheritance of desired traits in organisms** (for example, research and summarize the influence of humans on genetic outcomes in artificial selection—such as genetic modification, animal husbandry, or gene therapy—and the influence these technologies have had on society as well as the technologies that led to these scientific discoveries).
Score 2.0	**MS-LS4-4**—The student will:
	• Recognize or recall specific vocabulary (for example, *continuation of species, environment, genetic variation, natural selection, population, probability, reproduce, survive, trait*).
	• Describe how genetic variations of traits in a population increase some individuals' probability of surviving and reproducing.
	MS-LS4-5—The student will:
	• Recognize or recall specific vocabulary (for example, *animal husbandry, artificial selection, gene therapy, genetic modification, genetic outcome, influence, inheritance, organism, society, technology, trait*).
	• Describe technologies that allow humans to influence the inheritance of desired traits.
	• Describe the impacts these technologies have had on society.

Grade 3	
Score 3.0	The student will:
	3-LS4-2—**Use evidence to construct an explanation for how the variations in characteristics among individuals of the same species may provide advantages in surviving, finding mates, and reproducing** (for example, use observations and patterns to explain how variations in traits among individuals of the same species may provide advantages in survival and reproduction—such as plants that have larger thorns than other plants may be less likely to be eaten by predators or animals that have better camouflage coloration than other animals may be more likely to survive and produce offspring).
Score 2.0	**3-LS4-2**—The student will:
	• Recognize or recall specific vocabulary (for example, *advantage, camouflage, characteristic, coloration, environment, mate, offspring, organism, predator, relationship, reproduce, species, survive, variation*).
	• Describe variations in traits among organisms in a group.
	• Describe the relationship between particular traits and survival in particular environments.

Fossils

	Middle School	
Score 4.0	In addition to score 3.0 performance, the student demonstrates in-depth inferences and applications that go beyond what was taught.	
	Score 3.5	*In addition to score 3.0 performance, partial success at score 4.0 content*
Score 3.0	The student will: **MS-LS4-1—Analyze and interpret data for patterns in the fossil record that document the existence, diversity, extinction, and change of life forms throughout the history of life on Earth under the assumption that natural laws operate today as in the past** (for example, analyze and interpret data to identify patterns of changes in the level of complexity of anatomical structures in organisms and the chronological order of fossil appearance in rock layers).	
	Score 2.5	*No major errors or omissions regarding score 2.0 content, and partial success at score 3.0 content*
Score 2.0	**MS-LS4-1—**The student will: • Recognize or recall specific vocabulary (for example, *anatomical structure, assumption, chronological order, diversity, existence, extinction, fossil, fossil appearance, fossil record, history of life, level of complexity, life form, natural law, organism, pattern, rock layer, rock sequence*). • Describe changes in the level of complexity of anatomical structures in organisms. • Describe the chronological order of fossils.	
	Score 1.5	*Partial success at score 2.0 content, and major errors or omissions regarding score 3.0 content*
Score 1.0	With help, partial success at score 2.0 content and score 3.0 content	
	Score 0.5	*With help, partial success at score 2.0 content but not at score 3.0 content*
Score 0.0	Even with help, no success	
	Grade 3	
Score 3.0	The student will: **3-LS4-1—Analyze and interpret data from fossils to provide evidence of the organisms and the environments in which they lived long ago** (for example, analyze and interpret the type, size, and distribution of fossil organisms—such as marine fossils found on dry land or tropical plant fossils found in Arctic areas as well as fossils of extinct organisms—to defend claims about the environments in which the organisms once lived).	
Score 2.0	**3-LS4-1—**The student will: • Recognize or recall specific vocabulary (for example, *Arctic, dinosaur, distribution, environment, extinct, fossil, marine, organism, size, tropical, type*). • Describe fossils and the environments in which they were found.	

Evidence of Common Ancestry

	High School	
Score 4.0	In addition to score 3.0 performance, the student demonstrates in-depth inferences and applications that go beyond what was taught.	
	Score 3.5	*In addition to score 3.0 performance, partial success at score 4.0 content*
Score 3.0	The student will: **HS-LS4-1—Communicate scientific information that common ancestry and biological evolution are supported by multiple lines of empirical evidence** (for example, communicate orally, graphically, or textually to give evidence for common ancestry and biological evolution—such as similarities in DNA sequences, anatomical structures, and the order of appearance of structures in embryological development—and to explain how each line of evidence relates to common ancestry and biological evolution).	

continued →

	Score 2.5	*No major errors or omissions regarding score 2.0 content, and partial success at score 3.0 content*
Score 2.0	**HS-LS4-1**—The student will: • Recognize or recall specific vocabulary (for example, *anatomical structure, biochemical characteristic, biological evolution, common ancestry, degree of kinship, development, DNA sequence, embryological, evidence for unity of life, order of appearance, origin of life, phylogenetics, shared characteristic, similarity, structure*). • Describe similarities in DNA sequences, anatomical structures, and order of appearance of structures in embryological development of various organisms. • Describe the process of biological evolution.	
	Score 1.5	*Partial success at score 2.0 content, and major errors or omissions regarding score 3.0 content*
Score 1.0	With help, partial success at score 2.0 content and score 3.0 content	
	Score 0.5	*With help, partial success at score 2.0 content but not at score 3.0 content*
Score 0.0	Even with help, no success	
Middle School		
Score 3.0	The student will: **MS-LS4-2**—**Apply scientific ideas to construct an explanation for the anatomical similarities and differences among modern organisms and between modern and fossil organisms to infer evolutionary relationships** (for example, use scientific ideas to explain the evolutionary relationships among organisms in terms of similarities or differences of gross appearance of anatomical structures). **MS-LS4-3**—**Analyze displays of pictorial data to compare patterns of similarities in the embryological development across multiple species to identify relationships not evident in the fully formed anatomy** (for example, compare the macroscopic appearance of embryological development in diagrams and pictures to infer general patterns of relatedness among embryos of different organisms).	
Score 2.0	**MS-LS4-2**—The student will: • Recognize or recall specific vocabulary (for example, *anatomical, appearance, difference, evolutionary, fossil, fossil evidence, modern, organism, relationship, similarity, unity of life*). • Describe anatomical similarities and differences between modern and fossil organisms. **MS-LS4-3**—The student will: • Recognize or recall specific vocabulary (for example, *anatomy, appearance, development, embryo, embryological, macroscopic, organism, pattern, relatedness, relationship, similarity, species*). • Describe macroscopic similarities among different organisms in embryological development.	

Earth and Space Sciences

The Solar System

	High School	
Score 4.0	In addition to score 3.0 performance, the student demonstrates in-depth inferences and applications that go beyond what was taught.	
	Score 3.5	*In addition to score 3.0 performance, partial success at score 4.0 content*
Score 3.0	The student will: **HS-ESS1-4—Use mathematical or computational representations to predict the motion of orbiting objects in the solar system** (for example, apply mathematical or computational representations for the gravitational attraction of bodies and the Newtonian gravitational laws of orbital motions to predict the motion of orbiting objects—such as human-made satellites, planets, and moons—in the solar system).	
	Score 2.5	*No major errors or omissions regarding score 2.0 content, and partial success at score 3.0 content*
Score 2.0	**HS-ESS1-4**—The student will: • Recognize or recall specific vocabulary (for example, *attraction, gravitational, moon, motion, Newtonian gravitational laws, orbit, orbital motion, planet, predict, satellite, solar system, space probe*). • Describe how objects orbit around other objects. • Describe the key parts of Newton's gravitational laws of orbital motions.	
	Score 1.5	*Partial success at score 2.0 content, and major errors or omissions regarding score 3.0 content*
Score 1.0	With help, partial success at score 2.0 content and score 3.0 content	
	Score 0.5	*With help, partial success at score 2.0 content but not at score 3.0 content*
Score 0.0	Even with help, no success	
	Middle School	
Score 3.0	The student will: **MS-ESS1-1—Develop and use a model of the Earth-sun-moon system to describe the cyclic patterns of lunar phases, eclipses of the sun and moon, and seasons** (for example, create and use a physical, graphical, or conceptual model to describe the cycling of lunar phases, solar and lunar eclipses, and the seasons). **MS-ESS1-2—Develop and use a model to describe the role of gravity in the motions within galaxies and the solar system** (for example, create and use a physical model [such as an analogy of distance along a football field or a computer visualization of elliptical orbits] or a conceptual model [such as a mathematical proportion relative to the size of a familiar object such as a student's school or state] to explain that gravity is the force that holds together the solar system and Milky Way galaxy and that gravity controls the orbital motions within both). **MS-ESS1-3—Analyze and interpret data to determine scale properties of objects in the solar system** (for example, analyze and interpret statistical information, drawings, photographs, and models from Earth-based instruments, space-based telescopes, and spacecrafts to determine similarities and differences based on scale properties among solar system objects, such as the sizes of an object's orbital radius, its volcanoes and other surface features, and its crust, atmosphere, and other layers).	

continued →

Score 2.0	**MS-ESS1-1**—The student will:
	• Recognize or recall specific vocabulary (for example, *cycle, cyclic, Earth-sun-moon system, eclipse, lunar eclipse, lunar phase, motion, pattern, season, solar eclipse*).
	• Describe the lunar phases.
	• Describe solar and lunar eclipses.
	• Describe how the seasons are created.
	MS-ESS1-2—The student will:
	• Recognize or recall specific vocabulary (for example, *asteroid movement pattern, comet, comet movement pattern, elliptical orbit, force, galaxy, gravity, meteor movement pattern, Milky Way, motion, orbit, orbital motion, planet orbit, solar system*).
	• Describe the role of gravity in the motions within galaxies and the solar system.
	MS-ESS1-3—The student will:
	• Recognize or recall specific vocabulary (for example, *atmosphere, crust, Earth-based, instrument, layer, orbital radius, planet composition, planet orbit, planet size, scale property, solar system, space-based, spacecraft, surface feature, telescope*).
	• Describe the scale properties of various objects in the solar system.

Grade 5	
Score 3.0	The student will:
	5-ESS1-2—**Represent data in graphical displays to reveal patterns of daily changes in length and direction of shadows, day and night, and the seasonal appearance of some stars in the night sky** (for example, display data in a bar graph, pictograph, or pie chart to reveal patterns of daily changes, such as the position and motion of Earth with respect to the sun, the length and direction of shadows, the length of day and night, and the seasonal appearance of some stars in the night sky).
Score 2.0	**5-ESS1-2**—The student will:
	• Recognize or recall specific vocabulary (for example, *appearance, change, daily, direction, Earth's axis, Earth's orbit, length, motion, night sky, pattern, position, seasonal, shadow, star, visible*).
	• Plot data about the length and direction of shadows, length of day and night, and seasonal appearance of stars in a graph.

Grade 1	
Score 3.0	The student will:
	1-ESS1-2—**Make observations at different times of year to relate the amount of daylight to the time of year** (for example, use observations—firsthand or from media—to make relative comparisons of the amount of daylight in the winter to the amount in the spring or fall).
Score 2.0	**1-ESS1-2**—The student will:
	• Recognize or recall specific vocabulary (for example, *comparison, daylight, fall, observation, spring, summer, sun's position, sun's size, sunrise, sunset, winter, year*).
	• Make and record observations of the amount of sunlight at different times of the year.

The Universe and Stars

High School		
Score 4.0	In addition to score 3.0 performance, the student demonstrates in-depth inferences and applications that go beyond what was taught.	
	Score 3.5	*In addition to score 3.0 performance, partial success at score 4.0 content*
Score 3.0	The student will: **HS-ESS1-1—Develop a model based on evidence to illustrate the life span of the sun and the role of nuclear fusion in the sun's core to release energy in the form of radiation** (for example, use evidence—such as observations of the masses and lifetimes of other stars as well as the ways that the sun's radiation varies due to sudden solar flares, the eleven-year sunspot cycle, and non-cyclic variations over centuries—to create a model that illustrates the energy transfer mechanisms that allow energy from nuclear fusion in the sun's core to reach Earth). **HS-ESS1-2—Construct an explanation of the Big Bang theory based on astronomical evidence of light spectra, motion of distant galaxies, and composition of matter in the universe** (for example, explain and defend the Big Bang theory using astronomical evidence, such as the red shift of light from galaxies as an indication that the universe is currently expanding, the cosmic microwave background as the remnant radiation from the Big Bang, and the observed composition—three-fourths hydrogen and one-fourth helium—of ordinary matter found in stars and interstellar gases matching that predicted by the Big Bang theory). **HS-ESS1-3—Communicate scientific ideas about the way stars, over their life cycle, produce elements** (for example, use speech, graphs, text, and mathematics to communicate scientific ideas about the way nucleosynthesis, and therefore the creation of different elements, varies as a function of the mass of a star and its life stage).	
	Score 2.5	*No major errors or omissions regarding score 2.0 content, and partial success at score 3.0 content*
Score 2.0	**HS-ESS1-1**—The student will: <ul><li>Recognize or recall specific vocabulary (for example, *energy, life span, lifetime, mass, non-cyclic, nuclear fusion, radiation, release, solar flare, star, sun's core, sun's radiation, sunspot cycle, transfer, variation*).</li><li>Describe how a star's radiation varies over the life span of the star.</li><li>Describe how the process of nuclear fusion in the sun's core creates energy.</li><li>Describe how energy from the sun reaches Earth.</li></ul> **HS-ESS1-2**—The student will: <ul><li>Recognize or recall specific vocabulary (for example, *age of the universe, astronomical, Big Bang theory, composition, composition of the universe, cosmic microwave background, evidence for the Big Bang theory, evidence for the expansion of the universe, expand, galaxy, gas, helium, history of the universe, hydrogen, interstellar, light year, matter, motion, origin of the universe, radiation, red shift, remnant, solar system formation, spectrum, star, stellar, universe*).</li><li>Summarize the Big Bang theory.</li><li>Describe the evidence that supports the Big Bang theory.</li></ul> **HS-ESS1-3**—The student will: <ul><li>Recognize or recall specific vocabulary (for example, *element, function, life cycle, life stage, mass, nucleosynthesis, star, star composition, star destruction, star formation, star size, star temperature, star type*).</li><li>Describe how the process of nucleosynthesis creates different elements.</li><li>Describe how the process of nucleosynthesis varies due to the mass of the star and its life stage.</li></ul>	
	Score 1.5	*Partial success at score 2.0 content, and major errors or omissions regarding score 3.0 content*
Score 1.0	With help, partial success at score 2.0 content and score 3.0 content	
	Score 0.5	*With help, partial success at score 2.0 content but not at score 3.0 content*
Score 0.0	Even with help, no success	

continued →

Grade 5	
Score 3.0	The student will: **5-ESS1-1—Support an argument that differences in the apparent brightness of the sun compared to other stars is due to their relative distances from Earth** (for example, defend the claim that some stars seem brighter than others because of their relative distances from Earth, rather than their size).
Score 2.0	**5-ESS1-1**—The student will: • Recognize or recall specific vocabulary (for example, *apparent, astronomical distance, astronomical object, astronomical size, brightness, celestial body, distance, relative, star*). • Identify the distances of different stars (including the sun) from the Earth. • Describe the apparent brightness of various stars.
Grade 1	
Score 3.0	The student will: **1-ESS1-1—Use observations of the sun, moon, and stars to describe patterns that can be predicted** (for example, make observations—firsthand or from media—of the sun, moon, and stars to identify predictable patterns, such as the visibility of stars other than our sun at night but not during the day; the consistent movement of the sun and moon appearing to rise in one part of the sky, cross the sky, and set in an opposite part of the sky; and so on).
Score 2.0	**1-ESS1-1**—The student will: • Recognize or recall specific vocabulary (for example, *apparent movement of stars, apparent movement of the sun, day, Earth's rotation, moon, night, pattern, position, predict, predictable, rise, sky, star, sun, visible*). • State accurate information about the sun, moon, and stars. • Identify the relative positions of the sun, moon, and stars.

Weather and Climate

High School		
Score 4.0	In addition to score 3.0 performance, the student demonstrates in-depth inferences and applications that go beyond what was taught.	
	Score 3.5	*In addition to score 3.0 performance, partial success at score 4.0 content*
Score 3.0	The student will: **HS-ESS2-4—Use a model to describe how variations in the flow of energy into and out of Earth's systems result in changes in climate** (for example, use a model to explain how changes in surface temperatures, precipitation patterns, glacial ice volumes, sea levels, and biosphere distribution are caused by variations in the flow of energy into and out of Earth systems, and explain that these changes differ by timescale, ranging from changes that occur over the period of a decade to changes that occur over hundreds of millions of years).	
	Score 2.5	*No major errors or omissions regarding score 2.0 content, and partial success at score 3.0 content*
Score 2.0	**HS-ESS2-4**—The student will: • Recognize or recall specific vocabulary (for example, *biosphere, circulation, climate change, distribution, Earth system, energy, flow, glacial, ice volume, orbit, orientation, pattern, precipitation, sea level, solar output, surface temperature, timescale, variation, volcanic eruption*). • Describe the flow of energy into and out of Earth systems. • Describe the relationship between energy in Earth systems and changes in climate. • Describe how changes in climate may occur over different lengths of time.	
	Score 1.5	*Partial success at score 2.0 content, and major errors or omissions regarding score 3.0 content*

Score 1.0	With help, partial success at score 2.0 content and score 3.0 content	
	Score 0.5	*With help, partial success at score 2.0 content but not at score 3.0 content*
Score 0.0	Even with help, no success	

	Middle School	

Score 3.0	The student will:
	MS-ESS2-5—Collect data to provide evidence for how the motions and complex interactions of air masses results in changes in weather conditions (for example, use student-collected laboratory experiment data or teacher-provided data [such as weather maps, diagrams, and visualizations] as evidence for how weather can be predicted within probabilistic ranges; for instance, air masses flow from regions of high pressure to low pressure causing weather [defined by temperature, pressure, humidity, precipitation, and wind] at a fixed location to change over time, and sudden changes in weather can result when different air masses collide).
	MS-ESS2-6—Develop and use a model to describe how unequal heating and rotation of the Earth cause patterns of atmospheric and oceanic circulation that determine regional climates (for example, create a diagram, map, globe, or digital representation to explain how patterns of atmospheric circulation [such as sunlight-driven latitudinal banding, the Coriolis effect, and resulting prevailing winds] and oceanic circulation [such as the transfer of heat by the global ocean convection cycle, which is constrained by the Coriolis effect and the outlines of continents] vary by latitude, altitude, and geographic land distribution).

Score 2.0	**MS-ESS2-5**—The student will:
	• Recognize or recall specific vocabulary (for example, *air mass, air mass circulation, collide, condensation, flow, high pressure, humidity, interaction, low pressure, motion, precipitation, predict, pressure, probabilistic, range, temperature, weather condition, weather map, wind*).
	• Describe the relationship between weather conditions and the motions and interactions of air masses.
	MS-ESS2-6—The student will:
	• Recognize or recall specific vocabulary (for example, *altitude, atmospheric circulation, climate, climate pattern, constrain, continent, Coriolis effect, Earth's climate, geographic, global ocean convection cycle, heat, land distribution, latitude, latitudinal banding, oceanic circulation, prevailing, regional, rotation, sunlight-driven, unequal, unequal heating of air, unequal heating of land mass, unequal heating of oceans*).
	• Describe the relationship between heating of the Earth, rotation of the Earth, and climate.

	Grade 3	

Score 3.0	The student will:
	3-ESS2-1—Represent data in tables and graphical displays to describe typical weather conditions expected during a particular season (for example, represent average temperature, precipitation, and wind direction in pictographs and bar graphs in order to describe typical weather conditions expected during a particular season).
	3-ESS2-2—Obtain and combine information to describe climates in different regions of the world (for example, gather and synthesize information from books and other reliable media to describe the range of typical weather conditions, as well as the extent to which those conditions vary over time, in different regions of the world).

Score 2.0	**3-ESS2-1**—The student will:
	• Recognize or recall specific vocabulary (for example, *average, Celsius, Fahrenheit, precipitation, season, temperature, typical, weather condition, wind direction*).
	• Describe the typical weather conditions expected during particular seasons.
	3-ESS2-2—The student will:
	• Recognize or recall specific vocabulary (for example, *climate, region, typical, vary, weather condition*).
	• State accurate information about climates in different regions of the world.

continued →

Kindergarten	
Score 3.0	The student will: **K-ESS2-1—Use and share observations of local weather conditions to describe patterns over time** (for example, make qualitative and quantitative observations of local weather conditions—such as describing the weather as sunny, cloudy, rainy, or warm or tallying the number of sunny, windy, and rainy days in a month—to describe patterns over time; for instance, it is usually cooler in the morning than in the afternoon, the number of sunny days versus cloudy days varies from month to month, and so on).
Score 2.0	**K-ESS2-1**—The student will: • Recognize or recall specific vocabulary (for example, *afternoon*, *air movement*, *cloudy*, *cool*, *daily weather pattern*, *local*, *month*, *morning*, *rainy*, *seasonal change*, *seasonal weather*, *sunny*, *thermometer*, *warm*, *weather condition*, *weather pattern*, *windy*). • Make and record observations of local weather conditions.

Natural Hazards

Middle School		
Score 4.0	In addition to score 3.0 performance, the student demonstrates in-depth inferences and applications that go beyond what was taught.	
	Score 3.5	*In addition to score 3.0 performance, partial success at score 4.0 content*
Score 3.0	The student will: **MS-ESS3-2—Analyze and interpret data on natural hazards to forecast future catastrophic events and inform the development of technologies to mitigate their effects** (for example, distinguish natural hazards that can be reliably predicted [such as volcanic eruptions and severe weather] from natural hazards that occur suddenly and with no notice [such as earthquakes] and use their location and frequency to predict future events and design mitigating technologies, such as satellite systems, basements, or reservoirs).	
	Score 2.5	*No major errors or omissions regarding score 2.0 content, and partial success at score 3.0 content*
Score 2.0	**MS-ESS3-2**—The student will: • Recognize or recall specific vocabulary (for example, *catastrophic*, *drought*, *earthquake*, *flood*, *forecast*, *frequency*, *hurricane*, *location*, *mitigate*, *natural hazard*, *predict*, *reservoir*, *satellite*, *severe weather*, *technology*, *tornado*, *tsunami*, *volcanic eruption*). • Describe natural hazards. • Describe indicators that a natural hazard may occur. • Describe technologies that can mitigate the effects of natural hazards.	
	Score 1.5	*Partial success at score 2.0 content, and major errors or omissions regarding score 3.0 content*
Score 1.0	With help, partial success at score 2.0 content and score 3.0 content	
	Score 0.5	*With help, partial success at score 2.0 content but not at score 3.0 content*
Score 0.0	Even with help, no success	
Grade 4		
Score 3.0	The student will: **4-ESS3-2—Generate and compare multiple solutions to reduce the impacts of natural Earth processes on humans** (for example, design and critique different solutions to reduce the impact of natural hazards like earthquakes, floods, tsunamis, and volcanic eruptions on humans, such as by designing an earthquake-resistant building or by improving the monitoring of volcanic activity).	

Score 2.0	4-ESS3-2—The student will:
	• Recognize or recall specific vocabulary (for example, *earthquake, flood, impact, monitor, natural hazard, reduce, resistant, tsunami, volcanic activity, volcanic eruption*).
	• Describe the effects of various natural disasters.
	• Describe the impacts of natural hazards on humans.
Grade 3	
Score 3.0	The student will:
	3-ESS3-1—Make a claim about the merit of a design solution that reduces the impacts of a weather-related hazard (for example, judge the effectiveness of a design solution to a weather-related hazard, such as flood barriers, wind-resistant roofs, and lightning rods).
Score 2.0	3-ESS3-1—The student will:
	• Recognize or recall specific vocabulary (for example, *barrier, effective, flood, hazard, impact, lightning rod, reduce, resistant, weather-related, wind*).
	• Describe the impacts of a weather-related hazard.
	• Describe how a design solution reduces the impact of a weather-related hazard.
Kindergarten	
Score 3.0	The student will:
	K-ESS3-2—Ask questions to obtain information about the purpose of weather forecasting to prepare for, and respond to, severe weather (for example, ask questions to figure out why it is important to make predictions about local forms of severe weather).
Score 2.0	K-ESS3-2—The student will:
	• Recognize or recall specific vocabulary (for example, *forecast, local, prediction, prepare, purpose, region, respond, severe weather, weather forecasting*).
	• Describe local forms of severe weather.
	• Describe how to respond to severe weather situations.

Weathering and Erosion

	Grade 4	
Score 4.0	In addition to score 3.0 performance, the student demonstrates in-depth inferences and applications that go beyond what was taught.	
	Score 3.5	*In addition to score 3.0 performance, partial success at score 4.0 content*
Score 3.0	The student will:	
	4-ESS2-1—Make observations and/or measurements to provide evidence of the effects of weathering or the rate of erosion by water, ice, wind, or vegetation (for example, observe or measure the amount of vegetation, speed of wind, relative rate of deposition, angle of slope in the downhill movement of water, cycles of freezing and thawing of water, cycles of heating and cooling, or volume of water flow to give evidence of the effects of weathering and the rate of erosion).	
	Score 2.5	*No major errors or omissions regarding score 2.0 content, and partial success at score 3.0 content*
Score 2.0	4-ESS2-1—The student will:	
	• Recognize or recall specific vocabulary (for example, *angle, cool, cycle, deposition, downhill, erosion, erosion resistance, freeze, heat, ice, rate, relative, slope, soil erosion, speed, thaw, vegetation, volume, water, water flow, weathering, wind*).	
	• Describe the effects of weathering or erosion by water, ice, wind, or vegetation.	
	Score 1.5	*Partial success at score 2.0 content, and major errors or omissions regarding score 3.0 content*

continued →

Score 1.0	With help, partial success at score 2.0 content and score 3.0 content	
	Score 0.5	With help, partial success at score 2.0 content but not at score 3.0 content
Score 0.0	Even with help, no success	

Grade 2		
Score 3.0	The student will: **2-ESS2-1—Compare multiple solutions designed to slow or prevent wind or water from changing the shape of the land** (for example, compare different designs of dikes and windbreaks to hold back water and wind or different designs that use shrubs, grass, and trees to prevent erosion).	
Score 2.0	2-ESS2-1—The student will: • Recognize or recall specific vocabulary (for example, *dike, erosion, grass, land, prevent, rock, shrub, water, weather, weathering, wind, windbreak*). • Explain ways in which wind and water can change the shape of the land. • Describe how various solutions prevent wind and water from changing the shape of the land.	

Water and Earth's Surface

High School		
Score 4.0	In addition to score 3.0 performance, the student demonstrates in-depth inferences and applications that go beyond what was taught.	
	Score 3.5	In addition to score 3.0 performance, partial success at score 4.0 content
Score 3.0	The student will: **HS-ESS2-5—Plan and conduct an investigation of the properties of water and its effects on Earth materials and surface processes** (for example, use water and a variety of solid materials to plan and conduct a mechanical investigation [such as on stream transportation and deposition using a stream table, on erosion using variations in soil moisture content, or on frost wedging by the expansion of water as it freezes] or a chemical investigation [such as on chemical weathering and recrystallization by testing the solubility of different materials or on melt generation by examining how water lowers the melting temperature of most solids] to provide evidence for connections between the hydrologic cycle and system interactions commonly known as the rock cycle).	
	Score 2.5	No major errors or omissions regarding score 2.0 content, and partial success at score 3.0 content
Score 2.0	HS-ESS2-5—The student will: • Recognize or recall specific vocabulary (for example, *advection, chemical, deposition, Earth material, erosion, expansion, frost wedging, hydrologic cycle, interaction, mechanical, melt generation, moisture, property, recrystallization, rock cycle, solubility, stream table, surface process, system, transportation, weathering, wedge*). • Describe how the properties of water affect Earth materials. • Describe the relationship between the hydrologic cycle and the rock cycle.	
	Score 1.5	Partial success at score 2.0 content, and major errors or omissions regarding score 3.0 content
Score 1.0	With help, partial success at score 2.0 content and score 3.0 content	
	Score 0.5	With help, partial success at score 2.0 content but not at score 3.0 content
Score 0.0	Even with help, no success	
Middle School		
Score 3.0	The student will: **MS-ESS2-4—Develop a model to describe the cycling of water through Earth's systems driven by energy from the sun and the force of gravity** (for example, create a conceptual or physical model to explain how water changes state as it moves through the multiple pathways of the hydrologic cycle).	

Score 2.0	MS-ESS2-4—The student will:
	• Recognize or recall specific vocabulary (for example, *cycle*, *Earth system*, *energy*, *force*, *gravity*, *hydrologic cycle*, *percolation*, *water cycle*).
	• Describe each phase of the hydrologic cycle.

Grade 5	
Score 3.0	The student will:
	5-ESS2-2—Describe and graph the amounts and percentages of water and fresh water in various reservoirs to provide evidence about the distribution of water on Earth (for example, describe and graph the amounts [area and volume] and percentages of fresh water and overall water in various reservoirs on Earth [such as oceans, lakes, rivers, glaciers, groundwater, and polar ice caps] to provide evidence that most fresh water is in glaciers or underground, while only a tiny fraction is in streams, lakes, wetlands, and the atmosphere).
Score 2.0	**5-ESS2-2**—The student will:
	• Recognize or recall specific vocabulary (for example, *area*, *atmosphere*, *distribution*, *forms of water*, *fraction*, *fresh water*, *glacier*, *groundwater*, *lake*, *ocean*, *percentage*, *polar ice caps*, *properties of water*, *reservoir*, *river*, *stream*, *underground*, *variety*, *volume*, *water capacity*, *wetland*).
	• Identify the various sources of fresh water on Earth.
	• Describe the amounts and percentages of fresh water and overall water on Earth.

Grade 2	
Score 3.0	The student will:
	2-ESS2-3—Obtain information to identify where water is found on Earth and that it can be solid or liquid (for example, obtain information using various texts; text features, such as headings, tables of contents, glossaries, electronic menus, and icons; and other media to identify that water on Earth is found in oceans, rivers, lakes, and ponds and that it can exist as solid ice or in liquid form).
Score 2.0	**2-ESS2-3**—The student will:
	• Recognize or recall specific vocabulary (for example, *Earth*, *electronic menu*, *forms of water*, *glossary*, *heading*, *ice*, *icon*, *lake*, *liquid*, *ocean*, *pond*, *river*, *solid*, *table of contents*, *text feature*, *water*).
	• Describe the forms of water.
	• Identify sources of water (both liquid and solid) on Earth.

Earth's History

High School	
Score 4.0	In addition to score 3.0 performance, the student demonstrates in-depth inferences and applications that go beyond what was taught.
	Score 3.5 — *In addition to score 3.0 performance, partial success at score 4.0 content*
Score 3.0	The student will:
	HS-ESS1-6—Apply scientific reasoning and evidence from ancient Earth materials, meteorites, and other planetary surfaces to construct an account of Earth's formation and early history (for example, use available evidence within the solar system—such as the sizes and compositions of solar system objects, the impact cratering record of planetary surfaces, or the absolute ages of ancient materials obtained by the radiometric dating of meteorites, moon rocks, and Earth's oldest minerals—to reconstruct the early history of Earth, which formed along with the rest of the solar system 4.6 billion years ago).
	Score 2.5 — *No major errors or omissions regarding score 2.0 content, and partial success at score 3.0 content*

continued →

Score 2.0	HS-ESS1-6—The student will: • Recognize or recall specific vocabulary (for example, *ancient, composition, Earth material, Earth's formation, history, impact cratering, meteorite, mineral, moon rock, planetary, radiometric dating, record, solar system, surface*). • Describe key events from Earth's formation and early history.
	Score 1.5	*Partial success at score 2.0 content, and major errors or omissions regarding score 3.0 content*
Score 1.0	With help, partial success at score 2.0 content and score 3.0 content
	Score 0.5	*With help, partial success at score 2.0 content but not at score 3.0 content*
Score 0.0	Even with help, no success

Middle School

Score 3.0	The student will: **MS-ESS1-4—Construct a scientific explanation based on evidence from rock strata for how the geologic time scale is used to organize Earth's 4.6-billion-year-old history** (for example, use evidence to explain how rock formations and the fossils they contain [such as the formation of mountain chains and ocean basins, the evolution or extinction of particular living organisms, or significant volcanic eruptions] are used to establish relative ages of major events in Earth's history, which could range from being very recent [such as the last Ice Age or the earliest fossils of *Homo sapiens*] to very old [such as the formation of Earth or the earliest evidence of life]).
Score 2.0	MS-ESS1-4—The student will: • Recognize or recall specific vocabulary (for example, *Earth's age, evidence, evolution, extinction, formation, fossil, geologic, geologic evidence, history,* Homo sapiens, *Ice Age, living organism, mountain chain, ocean basin, relative, rock formation, rock layer movement, rock strata, sedimentary rock, time scale, volcanic eruption*). • Describe how the geologic time scale is used to organize major events in Earth's history.

Grade 4

Score 3.0	The student will: **4-ESS1-1—Identify evidence from patterns in rock formations and fossils in rock layers to support an explanation for changes in a landscape over time** (for example, identify patterns in rock formations and use these patterns to explain changes in a landscape over time; for instance, rock layers containing marine shell fossils above rock layers containing only plant fossils might indicate a gradual change from land to water, or a canyon with different rock layers in the walls and a river in the bottom might indicate that the river gradually cut through the rock).
Score 2.0	4-ESS1-1—The student will: • Recognize or recall specific vocabulary (for example, *canyon, change, fossil, gradual, landscape, marine, plant, prehistoric environment, river, rock formation, rock layer, shell*). • Describe patterns in rock formation and fossils.

Grade 2

Score 3.0	The student will: **2-ESS1-1—Use information from several sources to provide evidence that Earth events can occur quickly or slowly** (for example, use observations from media to make and defend the claim that Earth's events can occur quickly or slowly; for instance, volcanic explosions and earthquakes occur quickly compared to the erosion of rocks, which occurs slowly).
Score 2.0	2-ESS1-1—The student will: • Recognize or recall specific vocabulary (for example, *Earth event, earthquake, erosion, quickly, slowly, volcanic explosion*). • Identify examples of Earth events that occur quickly and slowly.

Plate Tectonics

High School		
Score 4.0	In addition to score 3.0 performance, the student demonstrates in-depth inferences and applications that go beyond what was taught.	
	Score 3.5	*In addition to score 3.0 performance, partial success at score 4.0 content*
Score 3.0	The student will:	
	HS-ESS1-5—Evaluate evidence of the past and current movements of continental and oceanic crust and the theory of plate tectonics to explain the ages of crustal rocks (for example, review evidence of the ages of oceanic crust increasing with distance from mid-ocean ridges [a result of plate spreading] and the ages of North American continental crust increasing with distance away from a central ancient core [a result of past plate interactions] to evaluate the ability of plate tectonics to explain the ages of crustal rocks).	
	HS-ESS2-3—Develop a model based on evidence of Earth's interior to describe the cycling of matter by thermal convection (for example, use maps of Earth's three-dimensional structure—obtained from seismic waves, records of the rate of change of Earth's magnetic field, and identification of the composition of Earth's layers from high-pressure laboratory experiments—to create both a one-dimensional model of Earth with radial layers determined by density and a three-dimensional model, which is controlled by mantle convection and the resulting plate tectonics).	
	Score 2.5	*No major errors or omissions regarding score 2.0 content, and partial success at score 3.0 content*
Score 2.0	**HS-ESS1-5**—The student will:	
	• Recognize or recall specific vocabulary (for example, *age, Alfred Wegener, ancient core, continental crust, crustal deformation, crustal plate movement, crustal rock, interaction, mid-ocean ridge, mountain building, ocean layer, oceanic crust, plate, plate boundary, plate collision, plate spreading, plate tectonics, sea-floor spreading, theory*).	
	• Summarize the theory of plate tectonics.	
	• Describe the relationship between movements of Earth's crust and the ages of crustal rock.	
	HS-ESS2-3—The student will:	
	• Recognize or recall specific vocabulary (for example, *composition, cycle, density, Earth's layers, interior, magnetic field, mantle, mantle convection, matter, one-dimensional, plate tectonics, pressure, radial, rate, seismic wave, thermal, three-dimensional*).	
	• Describe the structure of the Earth's interior.	
	• Describe how matter cycles by thermal convection.	
	Score 1.5	*Partial success at score 2.0 content, and major errors or omissions regarding score 3.0 content*
Score 1.0	With help, partial success at score 2.0 content and score 3.0 content	
	Score 0.5	*With help, partial success at score 2.0 content but not at score 3.0 content*
Score 0.0	Even with help, no success	
Middle School		
Score 3.0	The student will:	
	MS-ESS2-1—Develop a model to describe the cycling of Earth's materials and the flow of energy that drives this process (for example, create and use a model to explain the processes of melting, crystallization, weathering, deformation, and sedimentation, which act together to form minerals and rocks through the cycling of Earth's materials).	
	MS-ESS2-3—Analyze and interpret data on the distribution of fossils and rocks, continental shapes, and seafloor structures to provide evidence of the past plate motions (for example, analyze and interpret the similarities of rock and fossil types on different continents; the shapes of the continents, including continental shelves; and the locations of seafloor structures, such as ridges, fracture zones, and trenches to give evidence of past plate motions).	

continued →

Score 2.0	**MS-ESS2-1**—The student will: • Recognize or recall specific vocabulary (for example, *crystal, crystalline solid, crystallization, cycle, deformation, Earth material, energy, flow, formation, melt, mineral, recrystallization, sedimentation, weathering*). • Describe the role of melting, crystallization, weathering, deformation, and sedimentation in the formation of rocks and minerals. **MS-ESS2-3**—The student will: • Recognize or recall specific vocabulary (for example, *continent, continental shape, continental shelf, distribution, Earth's crust, fossil, fracture zone, geologic force, geologic shift, lithosphere, motion, plate, ridge, rock layer movement, seafloor structure, trench*). • Describe ways in which the Earth's surface has changed over time. • Describe how distribution of fossils, rocks, continental shapes, and seafloor structures give evidence of past plate motions.
Grade 4	
Score 3.0	The student will: **4-ESS2-2—Analyze and interpret data from maps to describe patterns of Earth's features** (for example, analyze and interpret topographic maps of the Earth's land and ocean floor as well as maps of the locations of mountains, continental boundaries, volcanoes, and earthquakes to describe patterns of Earth's features).
Score 2.0	**4-ESS2-2**—The student will: • Recognize or recall specific vocabulary (for example, *bedrock, continental boundary, earthquake, feature, land, mountain, ocean floor, pattern, topographic map, volcano*). • Use maps to describe different features on Earth.
Grade 2	
Score 3.0	The student will: **2-ESS2-2—Develop a model to represent the shapes and kinds of land and bodies of water in an area** (for example, create a diagram, drawing, physical replica, diorama, dramatization, or storyboard that represents the shapes and kinds of land and bodies of water in an area).
Score 2.0	**2-ESS2-2**—The student will: • Recognize or recall specific vocabulary (for example, *body of water, Earth material, land, landform, shape, types of landforms, types of bodies of water*). • Identify kinds of land and bodies of water in an area.

Earth Systems

High School		
Score 4.0	In addition to score 3.0 performance, the student demonstrates in-depth inferences and applications that go beyond what was taught.	
	Score 3.5	*In addition to score 3.0 performance, partial success at score 4.0 content*
Score 3.0	The student will: **HS-ESS2-1—Develop a model to illustrate how Earth's internal and surface processes operate at different spatial and temporal scales to form continental and ocean-floor features** (for example, create a model that shows how the appearance of land features [such as mountains, valleys, and plateaus] and ocean-floor features [such as trenches, ridges, and seamounts] are a result of both constructive forces [such as volcanism, tectonic uplift, and orogeny] and destructive mechanisms [such as weathering, mass wasting, and coastal erosion]).	

	HS-ESS2-2—Analyze geoscience data to make the claim that one change to Earth's surface can create feedbacks that cause changes to other Earth systems (for example, analyze data to claim that one change to Earth's surface can create feedbacks that change other Earth systems, including climate feedbacks [such as how an increase in greenhouse gases causes a rise in global temperatures that melts glacial ice, which reduces the amount of sunlight reflected from Earth's surface, increasing surface temperatures and further reducing the amount of ice] and system interactions [such as how the loss of ground vegetation causes an increase in water runoff and soil erosion, how the loss of wetlands causes a decrease in local humidity that further reduces the wetland extent, or how dammed rivers increase groundwater recharge, decrease sediment transport, and increase coastal erosion]).	
	Score 2.5	*No major errors or omissions regarding score 2.0 content, and partial success at score 3.0 content*
Score 2.0	**HS-ESS2-1—**The student will: • Recognize or recall specific vocabulary (for example, *coastal erosion, constructive, continental, destructive, feature, force, geologic time, geologic time scale, geological dating, internal process, mass wasting, mechanism, molten rock, mountain, ocean floor, ocean layer, orogeny, plateau, ridge, seamount, spatial scale, surface process, tectonic uplift, temporal scale, trench, valley, volcanism, weathering*). • Describe how different land and ocean-floor features form. • Describe how constructive and destructive forces work to form land and ocean-floor features. **HS-ESS2-2—**The student will: • Recognize or recall specific vocabulary (for example, *atmospheric change, climate, coastal, Earth system, erosion, feedback, feedback effect, glacial ice, global, greenhouse gas, groundwater recharge, humidity, interaction, runoff, sediment, surface, system, temperature, transport, vegetation, wetland*). • Describe how changes to the Earth's surface result in changes to other Earth systems.	
	Score 1.5	*Partial success at score 2.0 content, and major errors or omissions regarding score 3.0 content*
Score 1.0	With help, partial success at score 2.0 content and score 3.0 content	
	Score 0.5	*With help, partial success at score 2.0 content but not at score 3.0 content*
Score 0.0	Even with help, no success	
Middle School		
Score 3.0	The student will: **MS-ESS2-2—Construct an explanation based on evidence for how geoscience processes have changed Earth's surface at varying time and spatial scales** (for example, use evidence to explain how geoscience processes such as surface weathering and deposition by the movements of water, ice, and wind—especially geoscience processes that shape local geographic features—change Earth's surface at time and spatial scales that can be large, such as slow plate motions or the uplift of large mountain ranges, or small, such as rapid landslides or microscopic geochemical reactions, and how many geoscience processes usually behave gradually but are punctuated by catastrophic events, such as earthquakes, volcanoes, and meteor impacts).	
Score 2.0	**MS-ESS2-2—**The student will: • Recognize or recall specific vocabulary (for example, *catastrophic, deposition, Earth's layers, Earth's surface, earthquake, geochemical reaction, geographic feature, geoscience, igneous rock, landslide, metamorphic rock, meteor impact, microscopic, mountain range, plate motion, sediment deposition, sedimentary rock, sedimentation, spatial scale, surface, surface runoff, time scale, uplift, volcano, water cycle, weathering*). • Describe how long it takes for various geoscience processes to change the Earth's surface (for example, weathering, deposition, plate motion, uplift, landslides, earthquakes, volcanoes, and meteors).	

continued →

	Grade 5
Score 3.0	The student will: **5-ESS2-1—Develop a model using an example to describe ways the geosphere, biosphere, hydrosphere, and/or atmosphere interact** (for example, create a model that uses an example [such as the influence of the ocean on ecosystems, landform shape, and climate; the influence of the atmosphere on landforms and ecosystems through weather and climate; or the influence of mountain ranges on winds and clouds in the atmosphere] to describe how Earth's systems [the geosphere, biosphere, hydrosphere, and atmosphere] interact).
Score 2.0	5-ESS2-1—The student will: • Recognize or recall specific vocabulary (for example, *atmosphere, atmospheric composition, atmospheric layer, atmospheric pressure, biosphere, change in the Earth's surface, climate, cloud, Earth material, Earth system, Earth's temperature, ecosystem, gases of the atmosphere, geosphere, hydrosphere, influence, interact, landform, mountain range, ocean, weather, wind, wind pattern*). • Describe the critical elements of the geosphere, biosphere, hydrosphere, and atmosphere. • State accurate information about the ways in which the geosphere, biosphere, hydrosphere, and/or atmosphere interact.

Humans and Earth Systems

	High School
Score 4.0	In addition to score 3.0 performance, the student demonstrates in-depth inferences and applications that go beyond what was taught.
	Score 3.5 *In addition to score 3.0 performance, partial success at score 4.0 content*
Score 3.0	The student will: **HS-ESS3-1—Construct an explanation based on evidence for how the availability of natural resources, occurrence of natural hazards, and changes in climate have influenced human activity** (for example, use evidence to explain how the availability of natural resources [such as high concentrations of minerals or fossil fuels and access to fresh water and regions of fertile soils], natural hazards [from interior processes such as volcanic eruptions and earthquakes, surface processes such as tsunamis and soil erosion, and severe weather such as hurricanes, floods, and droughts], and climate change [such as changes to sea level and regional patterns of temperature and precipitation] have influenced human activity). **HS-ESS3-4—Evaluate or refine a technological solution that reduces impacts of human activities on natural systems** (for example, use scientific ideas and principles; logical arguments about economic, societal, environmental, and ethical factors; and empirical data on the impacts of human activities [such as the quantities and types of pollutants released, changes to biomass and species diversity, or areal changes in land surface use] to evaluate or refine a technological solution that reduces the impact of human activities on natural systems; for instance, examples for limiting future impacts could range from local efforts [such as reducing, reusing, and recycling resources] to large-scale geoengineering design solutions [such as altering global temperatures by making large changes to the atmosphere or ocean]).
	Score 2.5 *No major errors or omissions regarding score 2.0 content, and partial success at score 3.0 content*
Score 2.0	HS-ESS3-1—The student will: • Recognize or recall specific vocabulary (for example, *availability, climate, concentration, drought, earthquake, erosion, fertile, flood, fossil fuel, fresh water, human activity, hurricane, influence, interior process, mass migration, mineral, natural hazard, natural resource, population, precipitation, regional, river delta, sea level, severe weather, surface process, temperature, tsunami, volcanic eruption*). • Describe the relationship between the availability of natural resources, natural hazards, and changes in climate and human activity.

	HS-ESS3-4—The student will: <ul><li>Recognize or recall specific vocabulary (for example, *areal, atmosphere, biomass, diversity, economic factor, empirical data, environmental factor, ethical factor, geoengineering, human activity, impact, natural system, ozone, pollutant, recycle, resource, reuse, societal factor, species*).</li><li>Summarize a technological solution for reducing the impact of human activities.</li><li>Summarize the impacts of human activity on natural systems.</li></ul>
	Score 1.5 *Partial success at score 2.0 content, and major errors or omissions regarding score 3.0 content*
Score 1.0	With help, partial success at score 2.0 content and score 3.0 content
	Score 0.5 *With help, partial success at score 2.0 content but not at score 3.0 content*
Score 0.0	Even with help, no success
Middle School	
Score 3.0	The student will: **MS-ESS3-3—Apply scientific principles to design a method for monitoring and minimizing a human impact on the environment** (for example, examine human environmental impacts, assess the kinds of solutions that are feasible, and design and evaluate solutions that could reduce human impacts on the environment; for instance, possible solutions could address water usage, including the withdrawal of water from streams and aquifers or the construction of dams and levees; land usage, including urban development, agriculture, or the removal of wetlands; or pollution, including that of the air, water, or land).
Score 2.0	MS-ESS3-3—The student will: <ul><li>Recognize or recall specific vocabulary (for example, *agriculture, aquifer, construction, dam, environment, human impact, land usage, levee, minimize, monitor, pollution, stream, urban development, water usage, wetland*).</li><li>Describe how humans have impacted the environment.</li><li>Describe how possible solutions mitigate human impacts.</li></ul>
Grade 5	
Score 3.0	The student will: **5-ESS3-1—Obtain and combine information about ways individual communities use science ideas to protect the Earth's resources and environment** (for example, gather and synthesize information from books or other reliable media about ways individuals and communities use science to protect the Earth).
Score 2.0	5-ESS3-1—The student will: <ul><li>Recognize or recall specific vocabulary (for example, *community, environment, individual, protect, resource, science*).</li><li>Describe specific ways that science is used to protect the Earth's resources and environment.</li></ul>
Kindergarten	
Score 3.0	The student will: **K-ESS3-3—Communicate solutions that will reduce the impact of humans on the land, water, air, and/or other living things in the local environment** (for example, consider the effect of human acts—such as cutting trees to produce paper and using resources to produce bottles—on the local environment, and describe ways to reduce this impact, such as by reusing paper and recycling cans and bottles).
Score 2.0	K-ESS3-3—The student will: <ul><li>Recognize or recall specific vocabulary (for example, *air, environment, human, impact, land, living thing, local, recycle, reduce, resource, reuse, water*).</li><li>Identify ways humans have changed the environment.</li><li>Describe ways to reduce the impact of humans on the environment.</li></ul>

Biogeology

High School		
Score 4.0	In addition to score 3.0 performance, the student demonstrates in-depth inferences and applications that go beyond what was taught.	
	Score 3.5	*In addition to score 3.0 performance, partial success at score 4.0 content*
Score 3.0	The student will: **HS-ESS2-7—Construct an argument based on evidence about the simultaneous coevolution of Earth's systems and life on Earth** (for example, make and defend claims about the dynamic causes, effects, and feedbacks between the biosphere and Earth's other systems—whereby geoscience factors control the evolution of life, which in turn continuously alters Earth's surface—using evidence; for instance, photosynthetic life altered the atmosphere through the production of oxygen, which in turn increased weathering rates and allowed for the evolution of animal life; microbial life on land increased the formation of soil, which in turn allowed for the evolution of land plants; or the evolution of corals created reefs that altered patterns of erosion and deposition along coastlines, which in turn provided habitats for the evolution of new life forms).	
	Score 2.5	*No major errors or omissions regarding score 2.0 content, and partial success at score 3.0 content*
Score 2.0	HS-ESS2-7—The student will: • Recognize or recall specific vocabulary (for example, *atmosphere, biogeology, biosphere, cause, coastline, coevolution, coral, deposition, dynamic, Earth system, Earth's surface, effect, erosion, evolution, factor, feedback, geoscience, habitat, microbial, oxygen, photosynthesis, photosynthetic life, rate, reef, simultaneous, surface, weathering*). • Describe the relationship between the biosphere and other Earth systems.	
	Score 1.5	*Partial success at score 2.0 content, and major errors or omissions regarding score 3.0 content*
Score 1.0	With help, partial success at score 2.0 content and score 3.0 content	
	Score 0.5	*With help, partial success at score 2.0 content but not at score 3.0 content*
Score 0.0	Even with help, no success	
Kindergarten		
Score 3.0	The student will: **K-ESS2-2—Construct an argument supported by evidence for how plants and animals (including humans) can change the environment to meet their needs** (for example, make and defend the claim that plants and animals can change an environment to meet their needs by citing examples such as a squirrel digging in the ground to hide its food or tree roots breaking concrete).	
Score 2.0	K-ESS2-2—The student will: • Recognize or recall specific vocabulary (for example, *animal, change, environment, human, need, plant*). • State examples of ways in which humans, plants, or animals have changed the environment to meet their needs.	

Natural Resources

High School		
Score 4.0	In addition to score 3.0 performance, the student demonstrates in-depth inferences and applications that go beyond what was taught.	
	Score 3.5	*In addition to score 3.0 performance, partial success at score 4.0 content*
Score 3.0	The student will: **HS-ESS3-2—Evaluate competing design solutions for developing, managing, and utilizing energy and mineral resources based on cost-benefit ratios** (for example, use cost-benefit ratios to evaluate competing design solutions, and develop best practices for agricultural soil use; coal, tar sand, and oil shale mining; or petroleum and natural gas extraction in order to maximize the conservation, recycling, and reuse of resources—such as minerals and metals—when possible and to minimize impacts when it is not). **HS-ESS3-3—Create a computational simulation to illustrate the relationships among management of natural resources, the sustainability of human populations, and biodiversity** (for example, create a computational simulation and use it to describe the factors that affect the management of natural resources [such as costs of resource extraction and waste management, per-capita consumption, and the development of new technologies] and the factors that affect human sustainability and biodiversity [such as agricultural efficiency, levels of conservation, and urban planning]).	
	Score 2.5	*No major errors or omissions regarding score 2.0 content, and partial success at score 3.0 content*
Score 2.0	**HS-ESS3-2—**The student will: • Recognize or recall specific vocabulary (for example, *agricultural, conservation, cost-benefit ratio, develop, energy resource, extraction, harvesting of resources, impact, manage, metal, mineral, mineral resource, minimize, mining, natural gas, oil shale, petroleum, recycle, resource, reuse, soil use, tar sand, utilize*). • Summarize competing design solutions for developing, managing, and utilizing energy and mineral resources. • Describe the process of using cost-benefit ratios to evaluate design solutions. **HS-ESS3-3—**The student will: • Recognize or recall specific vocabulary (for example, *agricultural, biodiversity, conservation, consumption, efficiency, extraction, management, natural resource, per-capita, population, resource, sustainability, urban planning, waste management*). • Describe the relationship between natural resources, human populations, and biodiversity.	
	Score 1.5	*Partial success at score 2.0 content, and major errors or omissions regarding score 3.0 content*
Score 1.0	With help, partial success at score 2.0 content and score 3.0 content	
	Score 0.5	*With help, partial success at score 2.0 content but not at score 3.0 content*
Score 0.0	Even with help, no success	
Middle School		
Score 3.0	The student will: **MS-ESS3-1—Construct a scientific explanation based on evidence for how the uneven distributions of Earth's mineral, energy, and groundwater resources are the result of past and current geoscience processes** (for example, make and defend the claim that mineral and groundwater resources are limited, typically nonrenewable, and unevenly distributed as a result of removal by humans; for instance, uneven distributions of resources as a result of past processes include but are not limited to petroleum, which involves burial locations of organic marine sediments and subsequent geologic traps; metal ores, which involve locations of past volcanic and hydrothermal activity associated with subduction zones; and soil, which involves locations of active weathering or deposition of rock). **MS-ESS3-4—Construct an argument supported by evidence for how increases in human population and per-capita consumption of natural resources impact Earth's systems** (for example, using evidence from grade-appropriate databases on human populations and the rates of consumption of food and natural resources [such as fresh water, minerals, and energy], make and defend the claim that increases in human populations and per-capita consumption of natural resources have an impact on Earth's systems [such as changes to the appearance, composition, and structure of Earth's systems as well as the rates at which they change]).	

continued →

Score 2.0	**MS-ESS3-1**—The student will:
	• Recognize or recall specific vocabulary (for example, *deposition, distribution, energy source, geologic trap, geoscience, groundwater, hydrothermal, marine sediment, metal ore, mineral, nonrenewable, organic, petroleum, renewable, resource, subduction zone, volcanic, weathering*).
	• Describe the relationship between mineral resources and geoscience processes.
	• Describe how the distribution of various resources occurs.
	MS-ESS3-4—The student will:
	• Recognize or recall specific vocabulary (for example, *appearance, composition, consumption, Earth system, energy, fresh water, human population, impact, mineral, natural resource, per-capita, rate*).
	• Describe impacts of the increasing human population and consumption of natural resources.

Grade 4	
Score 3.0	The student will:
	4-ESS3-1—Obtain and combine information to describe that energy and fuels are derived from natural resources and their uses affect the environment (for example, gather and synthesize information to explain that energy and fuel come from renewable natural resources [such as energy generated from wind, water behind dams, and sunlight] and nonrenewable natural resources [such as fossil fuels and fissile materials] and that the use of these resources affects the environment in various ways, including loss of habitat due to dams or surface mining and air pollution from the burning of fossil fuels).
Score 2.0	**4-ESS3-1**—The student will:
	• Recognize or recall specific vocabulary (for example, *animal product, dam, energy, environment, fissile, fossil fuel, fuel, habitat, natural resource, nonrenewable, oil, pollution, renewable, resource, resource availability, sunlight, surface mining, water, wind*).
	• Identify examples of energy sources or fuels that come from natural resources.
	• Distinguish renewable resources from nonrenewable resources.
	• Explain ways that the use of energy and fuels affects the environment.

Kindergarten	
Score 3.0	The student will:
	K-ESS3-1—Use a model to represent the relationship between the needs of different plants or animals (including humans) and the places they live (for example, use a model to show that living things need water, air, and resources from the land and that they live in places that have the things they need; for instance, deer eat buds and leaves and therefore usually live in forested areas, grasses need sunlight so they often grow in meadows, and so on).
Score 2.0	**K-ESS3-1**—The student will:
	• Recognize or recall specific vocabulary (for example, *air, animal, human, land, living thing, need, plant, relationship, resource, water*).
	• Identify the needs of plants, animals, and humans.
	• Describe resources available in places where plants, animals, and humans live.

Global Climate Change

High School		
Score 4.0	In addition to score 3.0 performance, the student demonstrates in-depth inferences and applications that go beyond what was taught.	
	Score 3.5	*In addition to score 3.0 performance, partial success at score 4.0 content*
Score 3.0	The student will: **HS-ESS3-5—Analyze geoscience data and the results from global climate models to make an evidence-based forecast of the current rate of global or regional climate change and associated future impacts to Earth systems** (for example, analyze climate changes [such as changes to precipitation and temperature] and their associated impacts [such as those on sea level, glacial ice volumes, or atmosphere and ocean composition] to make and defend a claim about the current rate of global or regional climate change and a prediction of the associated future impacts to Earth systems). **HS-ESS3-6—Use a computational representation to illustrate the relationships among Earth systems and how those relationships are being modified due to human activity** (for example, use a computational model or simulation to show the relationships among the hydrosphere, atmosphere, cryosphere, geosphere, and biosphere, and explain how these relationships are modified due to human activity; for instance, an increase in atmospheric carbon dioxide results in an increase in photosynthetic biomass on land and in ocean acidification with resulting impacts on sea organism health and marine populations).	
	Score 2.5	*No major errors or omissions regarding score 2.0 content, and partial success at score 3.0 content*
Score 2.0	**HS-ESS3-5**—The student will: • Recognize or recall specific vocabulary (for example, *atmosphere, climate change, climate model, composition, Earth system, forecast, geoscience, glacial ice, global, impact, precipitation, rate, regional, sea level, temperature, volume*). • Describe evidence supporting global climate change. • Describe the causes and impacts of global climate change. **HS-ESS3-6**—The student will: • Recognize or recall specific vocabulary (for example, *acidification, atmosphere, atmospheric, biomass, biosphere, carbon dioxide, cryosphere, Earth system, geosphere, human activity, hydrosphere, marine, modify, organism, photosynthetic, population*). • Describe the relationships between hydrosphere, atmosphere, cryosphere, geosphere, and biosphere. • Describe how the relationships between Earth's systems are modified due to human activity.	
	Score 1.5	*Partial success at score 2.0 content, and major errors or omissions regarding score 3.0 content*
Score 1.0	With help, partial success at score 2.0 content and score 3.0 content	
	Score 0.5	*With help, partial success at score 2.0 content but not at score 3.0 content*
Score 0.0	Even with help, no success	
Middle School		
Score 3.0	The student will: **MS-ESS3-5—Ask questions to clarify evidence of the factors that have caused the rise in global temperatures over the past century** (for example, ask questions about tables, graphs, and maps of global and regional temperatures, atmospheric levels of gases such as carbon dioxide and methane, and the rates of human activities to clarify evidence of the factors that have caused the rise in global temperatures, including natural processes [such as changes in incoming solar radiation or volcanic activity] and, especially, human activities [such as fossil fuel combustion, cement production, and agricultural activity]).	
Score 2.0	**MS-ESS3-5**—The student will: • Recognize or recall specific vocabulary (for example, *agriculture, atmospheric, carbon dioxide, combustion, factor, fossil fuel, gas, global, human activity, methane, natural process, rate, regional, solar radiation, temperature, volcanic activity*). • Describe the different factors that have caused the rise in global temperature.	

Carbon Cycle

High School		
Score 4.0	In addition to score 3.0 performance, the student demonstrates in-depth inferences and applications that go beyond what was taught.	
	Score 3.5	*In addition to score 3.0 performance, partial success at score 4.0 content*
Score 3.0	The student will: **HS-ESS2-6—Develop a quantitative model to describe the cycling of carbon among the hydrosphere, atmosphere, geosphere, and biosphere** (for example, create a quantitative model of a biogeochemical cycle that includes the cycling of carbon through the ocean, atmosphere, soil, and biosphere—including humans—and use it to explain how carbon provides the foundation for all living organisms).	
	Score 2.5	*No major errors or omissions regarding score 2.0 content, and partial success at score 3.0 content*
Score 2.0	HS-ESS2-6—The student will: • Recognize or recall specific vocabulary (for example, *atmosphere, biogeochemical, biosphere, carbon, carbon cycle, Earth system, geosphere, hydrosphere, organism*). • Describe how carbon cycles through the hydrosphere, atmosphere, geosphere, and biosphere. • Describe the relationship between carbon and living organisms.	
	Score 1.5	*Partial success at score 2.0 content, and major errors or omissions regarding score 3.0 content*
Score 1.0	With help, partial success at score 2.0 content and score 3.0 content	
	Score 0.5	*With help, partial success at score 2.0 content but not at score 3.0 content*
Score 0.0	Even with help, no success	

Engineering

Defining Problems

	High School	
Score 4.0	In addition to score 3.0 performance, the student demonstrates in-depth inferences and applications that go beyond what was taught.	
	Score 3.5	*In addition to score 3.0 performance, partial success at score 4.0 content*
Score 3.0	The student will: **HS-ETS1-1—Analyze a major global challenge to specify qualitative and quantitative criteria and constraints for solutions that account for societal needs and wants** (for example, consider a major global challenge that can be addressed through engineering, such as the need for clean water and food or for energy sources that minimize pollution, and specify quantifiable and measurable criteria and constraints for a solution, such as satisfying any requirements set by society or taking issues of risk mitigation into account).	
	Score 2.5	*No major errors or omissions regarding score 2.0 content, and partial success at score 3.0 content*
Score 2.0	HS-ETS1-1—The student will: • Recognize or recall specific vocabulary (for example, *constraint, criteria, engineering, global challenge, measurable, need, qualitative, quantifiable, quantitative, requirement, risk mitigation, societal, solution*). • Summarize a major global challenge or problem. • Summarize societal needs and wants related to the challenge or problem.	
	Score 1.5	*Partial success at score 2.0 content, and major errors or omissions regarding score 3.0 content*
Score 1.0	With help, partial success at score 2.0 content and score 3.0 content	
	Score 0.5	*With help, partial success at score 2.0 content but not at score 3.0 content*
Score 0.0	Even with help, no success	
	Middle School	
Score 3.0	The student will: **MS-ETS1-1—Define the criteria and constraints of a design problem with sufficient precision to ensure a successful solution, taking into account relevant scientific principles and potential impacts on people and the natural environment that may limit possible solutions** (for example, precisely define a design task's criteria and constraints, including consideration of scientific principles and other relevant knowledge that limit possible solutions).	
Score 2.0	MS-ETS1-1—The student will: • Recognize or recall specific vocabulary (for example, *consideration, constraint, criteria, design problem, design task, environment, impact, limitation, possible, potential, precise, precision, principle, relevant, solution, sufficient*). • Describe the problem to be solved. • Describe scientific principles that are relevant to the problem. • Describe potential impacts on people and the natural environment.	

continued →

Grades 3–5	
Score 3.0	The student will: **3-5-ETS1-1—Define a simple design problem reflecting a need or a want that includes specified criteria for success and constraints on materials, time, or cost** (for example, define a simple design problem that includes constraints [available materials and resources that limit possible solutions to a problem] and criteria [the desired features of a solution that determine its success]).
Score 2.0	3-5-ETS1-1—The student will: • Recognize or recall specific vocabulary (for example, *available, constraint, cost, criteria, design problem, feature, limit, material, possible, problem, question formulation, resource, solution, specify, success, time*). • Identify criteria for success. • Identify constraints on solutions.
Grades K–2	
Score 3.0	The student will: **K-2-ETS1-1—Ask questions, make observations, and gather information about a situation people want to change to define a simple problem that can be solved through the development of a new or improved object or tool** (for example, approach a situation that people want to change or create a problem to be solved through engineering, and ask questions, make observations, and gather information to clarify the problem, understanding that a problem must be clearly understood before a solution can be designed).
Score 2.0	K-2-ETS1-1—The student will: • Recognize or recall specific vocabulary (for example, *change, clarify, design, development, improve, information, observation, problem, question, situation, solution, solve, tool*). • Identify the steps to defining the problem (for example, ask questions, make observations, and gather information). • Describe a simple problem.

Designing Solutions

High School	
Score 4.0	In addition to score 3.0 performance, the student demonstrates in-depth inferences and applications that go beyond what was taught.
	Score 3.5 *In addition to score 3.0 performance, partial success at score 4.0 content*
Score 3.0	The student will: **HS-ETS1-2—Design a solution to a complex real-world problem by breaking it down into smaller, more manageable problems that can be solved through engineering** (for example, break down criteria into simpler ones that can be approached systematically, and make tradeoffs—decisions about the priority of certain criteria over others—as needed).
	Score 2.5 *No major errors or omissions regarding score 2.0 content, and partial success at score 3.0 content*
Score 2.0	HS-ETS1-2—The student will: • Recognize or recall specific vocabulary (for example, *criteria, decision, engineering, manageable, priority, problem, solution, solve, systematic, tradeoff*). • Describe the smaller parts into which a complex problem might be broken.
	Score 1.5 *Partial success at score 2.0 content, and major errors or omissions regarding score 3.0 content*
Score 1.0	With help, partial success at score 2.0 content and score 3.0 content
	Score 0.5 *With help, partial success at score 2.0 content but not at score 3.0 content*
Score 0.0	Even with help, no success

Middle School	
Score 3.0	The student will: **MS-ETS1-2—Evaluate competing design solutions using a systematic process to determine how well they meet the criteria and constraints of the problem** (for example, use systematic processes for evaluating solutions, with respect to how well they meet the criteria and constraints of a problem, to evaluate competing solutions).
Score 2.0	**MS-ETS1-2—**The student will: • Recognize or recall specific vocabulary (for example, *competing, constraint, criteria, design solution, determine, evaluate, problem, process, solution, systematic*). • Describe the constraints and criteria of a problem. • Describe the systematic process used for evaluating solutions.
Grades 3–5	
Score 3.0	The student will: **3-5-ETS1-2—Generate and compare multiple possible solutions to a problem based on how well each is likely to meet the criteria and constraints of the problem** (for example, after researching a problem, test different solutions by investigating how well they perform under a range of likely conditions, and communicate with peers about proposed solutions, understanding that shared ideas can lead to improved designs).
Score 2.0	**3-5-ETS1-2—**The student will: • Recognize or recall specific vocabulary (for example, *communicate, condition, constraint, criteria, design, design process, improve, investigate, peer, performance, problem, propose, range, shared idea, solution*). • Describe the constraints of the problem and criteria for a successful solution.
Grades K–2	
Score 3.0	The student will: **K-2-ETS1-2—Develop a simple sketch, drawing, or physical model to illustrate how the shape of an object helps it function as needed to solve a given problem** (for example, convey a design solution through a sketch, drawing, or physical model in order to communicate problem-solving ideas to other people).
Score 2.0	**K-2-ETS1-2—**The student will: • Recognize or recall specific vocabulary (for example, *communicate, design solution, drawing, function, illustrate, model, physical model, problem, problem-solving idea, shape, sketch, teamwork*). • Describe how an object might function to solve a problem.

Evaluating and Testing Solutions

	High School	
Score 4.0	In addition to score 3.0 performance, the student demonstrates in-depth inferences and applications that go beyond what was taught.	
	Score 3.5	*In addition to score 3.0 performance, partial success at score 4.0 content*
Score 3.0	The student will: **HS-ETS1-3—Evaluate a solution to a complex real-world problem based on prioritized criteria and trade-offs that account for a range of constraints, including cost, safety, reliability, and aesthetics, as well as possible social, cultural, and environmental impacts** (for example, evaluate a solution to a complex real-world problem by taking into account a range of pre-specified constraints, including cost, safety, reliability, and aesthetics, and by considering social, cultural, and environmental impacts). **HS-ETS1-4—Use a computer simulation to model the impact of proposed solutions to a complex real-world problem with numerous criteria and constraints on interactions within and between systems relevant to the problem** (for example, use a computer to run simulations to test different ways of solving a problem to see which one is most efficient or economical and to make a persuasive presentation about how a given design will meet a client's needs).	
	Score 2.5	*No major errors or omissions regarding score 2.0 content, and partial success at score 3.0 content*
Score 2.0	**HS-ETS1-3—The student will:** • Recognize or recall specific vocabulary (for example, *aesthetic, consideration, constraint, cost, criteria, cultural, environmental, evaluate, impact, prioritize, problem, range, reliability, safety, social, solution, tradeoff*). • Describe constraints of a problem and the criteria for a successful solution. **HS-ETS1-4—The student will:** • Recognize or recall specific vocabulary (for example, *computer simulation, constraint, criteria, design, economical, efficient, impact, interaction, model, need, persuasive, presentation, problem, relevant, solution, solve, system*). • Describe proposed solutions.	
	Score 1.5	*Partial success at score 2.0 content, and major errors or omissions regarding score 3.0 content*
Score 1.0	With help, partial success at score 2.0 content and score 3.0 content	
	Score 0.5	*With help, partial success at score 2.0 content but not at score 3.0 content*
Score 0.0	Even with help, no success	
	Middle School	
Score 3.0	The student will: **MS-ETS1-3—Analyze data from tests to determine similarities and differences among several design solutions to identify the best characteristics of each that can be combined into a new solution to better meet the criteria for success** (for example, during the redesign process, identify the characteristics of the design that performed the best in each test—even if one design does not perform the best across all tests—to determine which characteristics should be incorporated into a new design or combined to create a solution that is better than any of its predecessors). **MS-ETS1-4—Develop a model to generate data for iterative testing and modification of a proposed object, tool, or process such that an optimal design can be achieved** (for example, develop various kinds of models to test the most promising solutions, and modify the designs based off the test results to continually refine a design solution until an optimal iteration can be achieved).	

Score 2.0	**MS-ETS1-3**—The student will:
	• Recognize or recall specific vocabulary (for example, *characteristic, combine, criteria, data, design, design solution, determine, difference, identify, incorporate, perform, predecessor, redesign process, similarity, solution*).
	• Describe similarities and differences of design solutions.
	MS-ETS1-4—The student will:
	• Recognize or recall specific vocabulary (for example, *data, design, design solution, iteration, iterative process, iterative testing, model, modification, modify, optimal, promising, propose, refine, solution, test result*).
	• Describe the purpose and need for iterative testing.
	• Describe the procedures for iterative testing.
Grades 3–5	
Score 3.0	The student will:
	3-5-ETS1-3—**Plan and carry out fair tests in which variables are controlled and failure points are considered to identify aspects of a model or prototype that can be improved** (for example, design and conduct tests to identify failure points or difficulties in various design solutions, with the failure points and difficulties identifying the elements of the design that need to be improved and ultimately determining which solution best solves the problem given the criteria and the constraints).
Score 2.0	**3-5-ETS1-3**—The student will:
	• Recognize or recall specific vocabulary (for example, *aspect, conduct, constraint, control, control of variables, controlled experiment, criteria, design, design solution, determine, difficulty, element, failure point, fair test, identify, improve, model, problem, prototype, replicable experiment, replicable result, solution, solve, test, variable*).
	• Carry out teacher-provided tests.
	• Describe the need for testing.
	• Describe testing procedures.
Grades K–2	
Score 3.0	The student will:
	K-2-ETS1-3—**Analyze data from tests of two objects designed to solve the same problem to compare the strengths and weaknesses of how each performs** (for example, test two different solutions to the same problem and compare their performances).
Score 2.0	**K-2-ETS1-3**—The student will:
	• Recognize or recall specific vocabulary (for example, *compare, data, design, different, perform, performance, problem, same, solution, solve, strength, test, weakness*).
	• Describe the purpose of testing.
	• Describe the strengths and weaknesses of each object in terms of solving the problem.

Appendix A: Using the New Taxonomy of Educational Objectives

The taxonomy presented here is part of a more comprehensive framework titled *The New Taxonomy of Educational Objectives* (Marzano & Kendall, 2007; see also Marzano & Kendall, 2008). Robert J. Marzano (2009) previously described the relationship between this taxonomy and designing and teaching learning goals and objectives in *Designing & Teaching Learning Goals & Objectives*.

As described in chapter 2 (page 25), the taxonomy includes four levels.

- ✦ Level 4 (Knowledge Utilization)
- ✦ Level 3 (Analysis)
- ✦ Level 2 (Comprehension)
- ✦ Level 1 (Retrieval)

To understand the taxonomy as it applies to academic content, it is necessary to address two types of knowledge: (1) declarative knowledge and (2) procedural knowledge. Declarative knowledge is informational content that can be conceptualized as a hierarchy in its own right. At the bottom of the declarative knowledge hierarchy is vocabulary—terms and phrases about which an individual has an accurate but not necessarily deep understanding. Facts reside a level above vocabulary terms and phrases. The highest level of the declarative knowledge hierarchy consists of generalizations, principles, and concepts.

Procedural knowledge includes mental procedures and psychomotor procedures. Both mental procedures and psychomotor procedures exist in a hierarchy as well. The lowest level of the mental procedure hierarchy contains single rules like those a writer might use when determining proper punctuation for an essay. The level immediately above single rules contains algorithms and tactics. A person will have an algorithm for multiplying two-digit numbers and a tactic (also known as a strategy) for how to read a bar graph. Macroprocesses reside at the highest level of the mental procedure hierarchy and can be thought of as arrays of single rules, algorithms, and tactics organized into an interacting set. For example, writing might best be described as a macroprocess. Psychomotor procedures also exist in a hierarchy. Foundational procedures like static strength, manual dexterity, and arm-hand steadiness are situated at the bottom of the hierarchy. A level up from foundational procedures are simple combination procedures like shooting a free throw in basketball. The highest psychomotor level involves complex combination procedures like guarding an opponent in basketball.

Level 1 (Retrieval)

The process of retrieval varies depending on the type of knowledge involved and the degree of processing required. There are three types of retrieval: (1) executing, (2) recalling, and (3) recognizing. The first two types apply to both declarative and procedural knowledge, while the third type applies only to procedural knowledge.

Recognizing Goals

Recognizing determines whether information is accurate or inaccurate. For example, a goal that requires students to select a synonym for a word from a word list relies on recognition. The teacher provides a synonym to the student, and the student must recognize its alternative. Examples of recognizing goals for the various types of knowledge include the following.

Declarative Knowledge: Students will be able to identify the sequence of critical events leading up to the outbreak of World War II in Europe.

Mental Procedures: Students will be able to identify a pie chart among a list of charts as appropriate for representing proportional data.

Psychomotor Procedures: Students will be able to acknowledge that cross-checking is an important defensive strategy in ice hockey.

Recalling Goals

Recalling requires students to produce information from permanent memory. Thus, a goal requiring students to produce a synonym for a specific term employs recall. This is more difficult than simply recognizing the correct example from a provided list. That is, recalling involves producing accurate information as opposed to simply recognizing it. Examples of recalling goals for the various types of knowledge include the following.

Declarative Knowledge: Students will be able to provide everyday examples that demonstrate the law of unbalanced forces.

Mental Procedures: Students will be able to recall that heart and breathing rates are components of a fitness assessment.

Psychomotor Procedures: Students will be able to recall that left-hand positioning and strength of grip are crucial aspects of playing the guitar.

Executing Goals

Executing refers only to procedural knowledge and involves actually carrying out a mental or psychomotor procedure, as opposed to simply recognizing or recalling information about it. To illustrate, consider the mental procedure of multicolumn subtraction. A teacher could write a recognizing goal for this procedure that requires students to identify accurate statements about multicolumn subtraction. The teacher could write a recalling goal that requires students to describe how to perform multicolumn subtraction. Neither goal actually asks a student to perform the process of multicolumn subtraction, however. This is the role of execution—asking a student to demonstrate a skill, strategy, or process.

There is a great deal of misunderstanding regarding executing goals, particularly as they relate to complex mental and psychomotor procedures. Although it is true that executing is at the lowest level of the taxonomy (because it is a form of retrieval), executing can be a difficult task for students, particularly when a complex mental or psychomotor procedure is involved. Consider the mental procedure of writing a persuasive essay. The actual execution of this process is a complex feat indeed, requiring the management of many interacting components. This is why writing is referred to as a macroprocess. The same can be said for the psychomotor procedure of playing basketball.

How, then, does one differentiate the level of difficulty for a complex procedure like writing? One way is to break the procedure into smaller component parts. For example, students less skilled at writing persuasive essays might focus on stating a clear claim and writing a few sentences to support the claim. Goals for students more skilled at constructing persuasive essays would incorporate additional components of the overall complex procedure into the process. For example, the more advanced students might also specify that each piece of evidence should be backed up with information supporting its validity.

Like writing a persuasive essay, playing basketball includes a variety of embedded procedures. For less skilled students, a goal might focus only on dribbling. A goal for more skilled students might include dribbling while running down the court and passing the ball to other players. Again, as the level of difficulty increases, the procedure involves more component procedures acting in tandem. Examples of executing goals for mental and psychomotor procedures include the following.

Mental Procedures: Students will be able to monitor and interpret heart rate and breathing rate.

Psychomotor Procedures: Students will be able to type at a reasonable speed using correct hand positioning.

Level 2 (Comprehension)

Comprehension processes require students to demonstrate an understanding of the overall structure of knowledge—the critical versus noncritical aspects of the knowledge. There are two related types of comprehension processes: (1) integrating and (2) symbolizing.

Integrating Goals

Integrating involves distilling knowledge down to its key characteristics and organizing the characteristics into a parsimonious, generalized form. Thus, integrating goals require students to describe the critical—as opposed to noncritical—information regarding content. Examples of integrating goals for the various types of knowledge include the following.

Declarative Knowledge: Students will be able to provide a description showing how the tilt and revolution of the Earth around the sun affects the seasons.

Mental Procedures: Students will be able to describe the key steps involved in selecting a random sample.

Psychomotor Procedures: Students will be able to explain the nuances of applying colors and forms in landscape painting when using a specific set of brush strokes.

Symbolizing Goals

Symbolizing requires students to translate their understanding into a graphic representation. In other words, symbolizing goals require students to translate what they have produced from an integrating goal into a nonlinguistic form. Consequently, symbolizing goals are frequently used in tandem with integrating goals. Examples of symbolizing goals for the various types of knowledge include the following.

Declarative Knowledge: Students will be able to graphically depict the relationship between supply and demand.

Mental Procedures: Students will be able to represent the flow of an information search on the Internet using text features and hierarchic structures in web-based information text.

Psychomotor Procedures: Students will be able to illustrate an S-turn, indicating the position of a skier's torso and skis relative to the fall line as well as the changing pressure on the uphill and downhill skis throughout the turn.

Level 3 (Analysis)

Analysis processes require students to go beyond what was actually taught in class to make inferences that create new awareness. There are five types of analysis processes: (1) matching, (2) classifying, (3) analyzing errors, (4) generalizing, and (5) specifying.

Matching Goals

Matching involves identifying similarities and differences. Examples of matching goals for the various types of knowledge include the following.

Declarative Knowledge: Students will be able to describe the similarities and differences between the terms *power* and *authority*.

Mental Procedures: Students will be able to describe what is similar and different about the processes of determining the validity of a primary source and a secondary source.

Psychomotor Procedures: Students will be able to describe how using a graphite pencil is similar to and different from using a charcoal pencil when sketching a face.

Classifying Goals

Classifying goes beyond organizing items into groups or categories (such an activity is better thought of as matching). Instead, classifying involves identifying the superordinate category into which knowledge belongs, as well as any subordinate categories. To illustrate, a goal that requires students to organize the fifty states into three categories based on voting tendencies in presidential elections (Democratic, Republican, or Independent) is considered a classifying task, because it requires students to identify the superordinate category to which each state belongs. Conversely, a learning goal that asks students to organize the fifty states into categories of their own choosing would be considered a matching goal, because it requires students to organize states by similarities and differences of their own design. Examples of classifying goals for the various types of knowledge include the following.

Declarative Knowledge: Students will be able to classify foods by their relative amounts of protein, fat, and vitamins.

Mental Procedures: Students will be able to identify gestures as a type of nonverbal communication.

Psychomotor Procedures: Students will be able to classify a set of strategies as common to net games as opposed to invasion games.

Analyzing Errors Goals

Analyzing errors requires students to identify factual or logical errors in declarative knowledge or processing errors in the execution of procedural knowledge. Examples of analyzing errors goals for the various types of knowledge include the following.

> **Declarative Knowledge:** Students will be able to identify what is plausible and implausible about the characters in a given story.

> **Mental Procedures:** Students will be able to identify flaws in graph presentation based on skill at interpreting the x and y axes.

> **Psychomotor Procedures:** Students will be able to identify technical errors in technique for a chosen instrument.

Generalizing Goals

Generalizing requires students to infer new generalizations or principles from known or stated information. Generalizing goals involve inductive thinking, in that students must create broad statements based on specific pieces of information. Examples of generalizing goals for the various types of knowledge include the following.

> **Declarative Knowledge:** Students will be able to make and defend generalizations about the influence of a source of information on the validity of the information presented.

> **Mental Procedures:** Students will be able to construct and defend generalizations about the use of specific refusal skills used in social situations.

> **Psychomotor Procedures:** Students will be able to generalize about the relationship between movement forms in sports and movement forms of machines mimicking those sports.

Specifying Goals

Specifying requires students to make and defend predictions about what might happen in a given situation. The process of specifying is deductive in nature, as it requires students to reason from a rule or principle to make and defend a prediction. Examples of specifying goals for the various types of knowledge include the following.

> **Declarative Knowledge:** Students will be able to identify circumstances that indicate the occurrence of processes that quickly or slowly change the Earth.

> **Mental Procedures:** Students will be able to make and defend inferences about measurement results based on an understanding of the relationship between perimeter and area.

> **Psychomotor Procedures:** Students will be able to make and defend inferences about the likely strategy of a tennis opponent when presented with consistent behaviors of the opponent.

Level 4 (Knowledge Utilization)

Knowledge utilization processes require students to apply or use knowledge in specific situations. There are four types of knowledge utilization processes: (1) decision making, (2) problem solving, (3) experimenting, and (4) investigating.

Decision-Making Goals

Decision making requires students to select among choices that initially appear equal. Examples of decision-making goals for the various types of knowledge include the following.

Declarative Knowledge: Students will be able to decide on the props and scenery for a stage setting of Denmark in the year 2050 based on an understanding of effective stage design.

Mental Procedures: Students will be able to decide, based on an understanding of specific learning strategies, the best way to learn new, personally chosen content.

Psychomotor Procedures: Students will be able to decide, based on an understanding of painting techniques, how to best create a specific visual effect.

Problem-Solving Goals

Problem solving requires students to accomplish a goal for which obstacles or limiting conditions exist. Problem solving and decision making are closely related in that decision making frequently serves as a subcomponent in the process of problem solving. However, whereas decision making does not involve obstacles to a goal, problem solving does. Examples of problem-solving goals for the various types of knowledge include the following.

Declarative Knowledge: Students will be able to propose a solution for the adoption of a specific alternative energy source based on an understanding of the obstacles and trade-offs associated with its use.

Mental Procedures: Students will be able to identify how best to solve a problem of negative social influence through an understanding of the best use of refusal skills.

Psychomotor Procedures: Students will be able to solve a specific fingering problem for the guitar by revising fingering notation to consider personal skills and limitations.

Experimenting Goals

Experimenting requires students to generate and test hypotheses about a specific physical or psychological phenomenon. Experimenting requires that the data are newly collected by students. That is, students must use data that they have generated themselves. Examples of experimenting goals for the various types of knowledge include the following.

Declarative Knowledge: Students will be able to generate and test a hypothesis that demonstrates an understanding of the possible impact of recent technology on society.

Mental Procedures: Students will be able to generate a hypothesis regarding which map projection will provide more and less accurate data about the distance between two places and test that hypothesis through measurement.

Psychomotor Procedures: Students will be able to generate and test a hypothesis about the ease or difficulty of using specific left-hand positions when playing a specific chord progression on the guitar.

Investigating Goals

Investigating requires students to examine a past, present, or future situation. Investigating is similar to experimenting in that it involves the gathering and testing of data. However, the data used in investigation are not gathered by direct observation on the part of the student (as they are in experimentation). Instead, the data used in investigation are assertions and opinions made by others. Investigating may be likened more to investigative reporting, whereas experimenting may be likened more to pure scientific inquiry. Examples of investigating goals for the various types of knowledge include the following.

Declarative Knowledge: Students will be able to investigate how acquiring daily food placed great demands on families in the 1800s.

Mental Procedures: Students will be able to investigate how specific methods of measuring weight have changed over time.

Psychomotor Procedures: Students will be able to investigate how and why changes in sports equipment can impact skill required for a specific sport.

Appendix B: Strategies for Setting an Effective Context for Learning

Engagement

Noticing When Students Are Not Engaged and Reacting	A teacher notes which students are not engaged and takes overt action to re-engage those students. Specific strategies include scanning the room, monitoring levels of attention, and measuring engagement.
Using Academic Games	A teacher uses inconsequential competition to maintain student engagement. Specific strategies include Classroom Feud, turning questions into games, and vocabulary review games.
Increasing Response Rates	A teacher maintains student engagement by using response-rate techniques during questioning. Specific strategies include response cards, paired or choral response, and elaborative interrogation.
Using Physical Movement	A teacher uses physical movement to keep students engaged. Specific strategies include body representations, drama-related activities, and asking students to stand up and stretch.
Maintaining a Lively Pace	A teacher maintains student engagement by using pacing techniques. Specific strategies include instructional segments, motivational hooks and launching activities, and pace modulation.
Demonstrating Intensity and Enthusiasm	A teacher models intensity and enthusiasm for the content being taught. Specific strategies include direct statements about the importance of content, nonlinguistic representations, and humor.
Using Friendly Controversy	A teacher maintains student engagement through the use of friendly controversy techniques. Specific strategies include class votes, seminars, and debates.
Providing Opportunities for Students to Talk About Themselves	A teacher provides students with opportunities to relate class content to their personal interests or lives. Specific strategies include interest surveys, student learning profiles, and informal linkages during class discussion.
Presenting Unusual Information	A teacher maintains student engagement by providing unusual or intriguing information about the content. Specific strategies include teacher-presented information, webquests, and guest speakers or firsthand consultants.

Rules and Procedures

Establishing Rules and Procedures	A teacher ensures effective execution of rules and procedures through a process of review. Specific strategies include using a small set of rules and procedures, generating rules and procedures as a class, and modifying rules and procedures with students.
Organizing the Physical Layout of the Classroom	A teacher arranges his or her classroom so that it facilitates movement and a focus on learning. Specific strategies include displaying student work and planning areas for learning centers, group work, and whole-class instruction.
Demonstrating "Withitness"	A teacher displays "withitness" (or classroom awareness) to maintain adherence to rules and procedures. Specific strategies include occupying the whole room physically and visually, being proactive, and noticing potential problems.
Acknowledging Adherence to Rules and Procedures	A teacher consistently praises students or classes that follow the rules or procedures. Specific strategies include verbal and nonverbal affirmations, tangible recognition, and daily recognition forms.
Acknowledging Lack of Adherence to Rules and Procedures	A teacher consistently applies consequences to students who fail to follow the rules or procedures. Specific strategies include verbal cues, nonverbal cues, and overcorrection.

Relationships

Using Verbal and Nonverbal Behaviors That Indicate Affection for Students	A teacher indicates affection for students through verbal and nonverbal cues. Specific strategies include greeting students at the classroom door, informal conferences or scheduled interactions, and giving students special responsibilities or leadership roles in the classroom.
Understanding Students' Interests and Backgrounds	A teacher produces a climate of acceptance and creates community by showing interest in students' interests and backgrounds. Specific strategies include student background surveys, teacher-student and parent-teacher conferences, and investigating student culture.
Displaying Objectivity and Control	A teacher maintains objectivity and control in his or her dealings with students. Specific strategies include self-reflection, identifying emotional triggers, and active listening and speaking.

Communicating High Expectations

Demonstrating Value and Respect for Reluctant Learners	A teacher actively demonstrates value and respect for reluctant learners. Specific strategies include identifying differential treatment of reluctant learners, using verbal and nonverbal indicators of respect and value, and identifying expectation levels for all students.
Asking In-Depth Questions of Reluctant Learners	A teacher actively engages reluctant learners in the classroom at the same rate as other students. Specific strategies include response opportunities, follow-up questioning, and encouragement.
Probing Incorrect Answers With Reluctant Learners	A teacher treats the questioning responses of reluctant learners and other students similarly. Specific strategies include using an appropriate response process, letting students "off the hook" temporarily, and answer revision.

References

Achieve. (n.d.a). *The case for Next Generation Science Standards.* Accessed at http://nextgenscience.org/case -next-generation-science-standards on February 26, 2015.

Achieve. (n.d.b). *Critical stakeholders.* Accessed at http://nextgenscience.org/critical-stakeholders on February 26, 2015.

Achieve. (n.d.c). *Development process.* Accessed at http://nextgenscience.org/development-process on February 26, 2015.

Achieve. (n.d.d). *Frequently asked questions.* Accessed at http://nextgenscience.org/frequently-asked-questions on February 26, 2015.

Achieve. (n.d.e). *International benchmarking.* Accessed at http://nextgenscience.org/international-benchmarking on February 26, 2015.

Achieve. (n.d.f). *Lead state partners.* Accessed at http://nextgenscience.org/lead-state-partners on February 26, 2015.

Achieve. (n.d.g). *States.* Accessed at http://nextgenscience.org/states-0 on February 26, 2015.

Achieve. (n.d.h). *Three dimensions.* Accessed at www.nextgenscience.org/three-dimensions on February 26, 2015.

Achieve. (n.d.i). *Writing team.* Accessed at http://nextgenscience.org/writing-team on February 26, 2015.

Achieve. (2010). *International science benchmarking report—Taking the lead in science education: Forging next-generation science standards.* Washington, DC: Author. Accessed at www.achieve.org/files /InternationalScienceBenchmarkingReport.pdf on February 26, 2015.

Achieve. (2013a). *DCI arrangements of the Next Generation Science Standards.* Washington, DC: Author. Accessed at www.nextgenscience.org/sites/ngss/files/NGSS%20DCI%20Combined%2011.6.13.pdf on February 26, 2015.

Achieve. (2013b). *How to read the Next Generation Science Standards (NGSS).* Accessed at www.nextgenscience .org/sites/ngss/files/How%20to%20Read%20NGSS%20-%20Final%2008.19.13.pdf on February 26, 2015.

Alexander, K. L., Entwisle, D. R., & Olson, L. S. (2007). Lasting consequences of the summer learning gap. *American Sociological Review, 72*(24), 167–180.

American Association for the Advancement of Science. (1993). *Benchmarks for science literacy.* New York: Oxford University Press.

American Association for the Advancement of Science. (2009). *Benchmarks for science literacy.* Accessed at http://www.project2061.org/publications/bsl/online/index.php on February 26, 2015.

Anderson, L. W., & Krathwohl D. R. (Eds.). (2001). *A taxonomy for learning, teaching, and assessing: A revision of Bloom's taxonomy of educational objectives* (Complete ed.). New York: Longman.

College Board. (2009). *Science: College Board standards for college success.* New York: Author. Accessed at https://professionals.collegeboard.com/profdownload/cbscs-science-standards-2009.pdf on February 26, 2015.

Colorado Department of Education. (2009). *Colorado academic standards: Science.* Denver, CO: Author. Accessed at www.cde.state.co.us/sites/default/files/documents/coscience/documents/science _standards_adopted_2009.pdf on February 26, 2015.

DeNavas-Walt, C., Proctor, B. D., & Smith, J. C. (2012). *Income, poverty, and health insurance coverage in the United States: 2011* (Report No. P60-243). Washington, DC: U.S. Government Printing Office. Accessed at www.census.gov/prod/2012pubs/p60-243.pdf on February 26, 2015.

Downing, S. M., & Haladyna, T. M. (Eds.). (2006). *Handbook of test development.* Mahwah, NJ: Erlbaum.

Fleischman, H. L., Hopstock, P. J., Pelczar, M. P., & Shelley, B. E. (2010). *Highlights from PISA 2009: Performance of U.S. 15-year-old students in reading, mathematics, and science literacy in an international context* (NCES 2011-004). Washington, DC: U.S. Government Printing Office. Accessed at http://nces.ed.gov/pubs2011/2011004.pdf on February 26, 2015.

Gillis, J. (2013, April 9). New guidelines call for broad changes in science education. *New York Times.* Accessed at www.nytimes.com/2013/04/10/science/panel-calls-for-broad-changes-in-science-education.html on February 26, 2015.

Haystead, M. W., & Marzano, R. J. (2009). *Meta-analytic synthesis of studies conducted at Marzano Research on instructional strategies.* Englewood, CO: Marzano Research.

Henderson, J. R. (2013). New science standards engineered for depth. *Education Update, 55*(11), 2–4.

Marzano, R. J. (2004). *Building background knowledge for academic achievement: Research on what works in schools.* Alexandria, VA: Association for Supervision and Curriculum Development.

Marzano, R. J. (2006). *Classroom assessment and grading that work.* Alexandria, VA: Association for Supervision and Curriculum Development.

Marzano, R. J. (2009). *Designing & teaching learning goals & objectives.* Bloomington, IN: Marzano Research.

Marzano, R. J. (2010). *Formative assessment and standards-based grading.* Bloomington, IN: Marzano Research.

Marzano, R. J., & Heflebower, T. (2012). *Teaching and assessing 21st century skills.* Bloomington, IN: Marzano Research.

Marzano, R. J., & Kendall, J. S. (2007). *The new taxonomy of educational objectives* (2nd ed.). Thousand Oaks, CA: Corwin Press.

Marzano, R. J., & Kendall, J. S. (2008). *Designing and assessing educational objectives: Applying the new taxonomy.* Thousand Oaks, CA: Corwin Press.

Marzano, R. J., & Pickering, D. J. (with Arredondo, D. E., Blackburn, G. J., Brandt, R. S., Moffett, C. A., Paynter, D. E., Pollock, J. E., et al.). (1997). *Dimensions of learning: Teacher's manual* (2nd ed.). Alexandria, VA: Association for Supervision and Curriculum Development.

Marzano, R. J., Rogers, K., & Simms, J. A. (2015). *Vocabulary for the new science standards.* Bloomington, IN: Marzano Research.

Marzano, R. J., Yanoski, D. C., Hoegh, J. K., & Simms, J. A. (with Heflebower, T., & Warrick, P.). (2013). *Using Common Core standards to enhance classroom instruction and assessment.* Bloomington, IN: Marzano Research.

Massachusetts Department of Education. (2006). *Massachusetts science and technology/engineering curriculum framework.* Malden, MA: Author. Accessed at www.doe.mass.edu/frameworks/scitech/1006.pdf on February 26, 2015.

Miller, J. D. (2010, February 21). *The public understanding of science in Europe and the United States.* Paper presented at the meeting of the American Association for the Advancement of Science, San Diego, CA.

Minnesota Department of Education. (2009). *Minnesota academic standards: Science K–12.* Accessed at www.scimathmn.org/stemtc/node/313 on February 26, 2015.

National Assessment Governing Board. (2008). *Science framework for the 2009 National Assessment of Educational Progress.* Washington, DC: Author. Accessed at www.nagb.org/publications/frameworks/science-09.pdf on February 26, 2015.

National Center for Education Statistics. (2012). *The nation's report card: Science 2011* (NCES 2012-465). Washington, DC: Institute of Education Sciences, U.S. Department of Education. Accessed at http://nces.ed.gov/nationsreportcard/pdf/main2011/2012465.pdf on February 26, 2015.

National Center for Injury Prevention and Control. (2012). *Understanding youth violence: Fact sheet.* Accessed at www.cdc.gov/violenceprevention/pdf/yv_factsheet2012-a.pdf on February 26, 2015.

National Governors Association Center for Best Practices & Council of Chief State School Officers. (2010a). *Common Core State Standards for English language arts & literacy in history/social studies, science, and technical subjects.* Washington, DC: Authors.

National Governors Association Center for Best Practices & Council of Chief State School Officers. (2010b). *Common Core State Standards for mathematics.* Washington, DC: Authors.

National Research Council. (1996). *National science education standards.* Washington, DC: National Academies Press.

National Research Council. (2012). *A framework for K–12 science education: Practices, crosscutting concepts, and core ideas.* Washington, DC: National Academies Press.

National Science Board. (2012). Industry, technology, and the global marketplace. In *Science and engineering indicators 2012* (pp. 1–74). Arlington, VA: National Science Foundation. Accessed at www.nsf.gov/statistics/seind12/pdf/c06.pdf on February 26, 2015.

NGSS Lead States. (2013). *Next Generation Science Standards: For states, by states.* Washington, DC: National Academies Press.

Organisation for Economic Co-operation and Development. (2012). *Education at a glance 2012: OECD indicators.* Paris: Author. Accessed at www.oecd.org/edu/EAG%202012_e-book_EN_200912.pdf on February 26, 2015.

Robelen, E. W. (2012, May 14). Who is writing the "Next Generation" Science Standards? [Web log post]. *Education Week.* Accessed at http://blogs.edweek.org/edweek/curriculum/2012/05/who_is_writing_the_next_genera.html on February 26, 2015.

Robelen, E. W. (2013, May 14). Common science standards face capacity issues. *Education Week.* Accessed at www.edweek.org/ew/articles/2013/05/15/31science.h32.html on February 26, 2015.

Rogers, K., & Simms, J. A. (2015). *Teaching argumentation: Activities and games for the classroom.* Bloomington, IN: Marzano Research.

Webb, N. L. (2006). Identifying content for student achievement tests. In S. M. Downing & T. M. Haladyna (Eds.), *Handbook of test development* (pp. 155–180). Mahwah, NJ: Erlbaum.

Wyoming State Board of Education. (2008). *Wyoming science content and performance standards.* Cheyenne, WY: Wyoming Department of Education. Accessed at http://edu.wyoming.gov/downloads/standards/Standards_2008_Science_PDF.pdf on February 26, 2015.

Index

MARZANO Research

Get a deeper understanding
of the new science standards

 Signature PD Service

Proficiency Scales for the New Science Standards Workshop

Since the release of the Next Generation Science Standards, educators have sought to make the new standards doable and meaningful in a classroom setting. Proficiency scales articulate progressions of knowledge and skills to help educators assess and track students' progress on the new standards. This workshop gives educators an in-depth understanding of how to weave proficiency scales for the NGSS into successful classroom practice.

Learning Outcomes

- Learn to write proficiency scales.

- Access hundreds of ready-made scales for the NGSS.

- Discover how to use proficiency scales to plan units and lessons, design effective formative assessments, and track students' progress.

- Acquire guidelines for addressing the scientific practices and for crosscutting concepts and disciplinary core ideas that compose each standard.

Learn more!
marzanoresearch.com/OnsitePD
888.849.0851